TAROT LORE AND OTHER B.S.

ALSO BY ESTELLE DANIELS

Astrologickal Magick
Weiser, 1995, York Beach, ME

Pocket Guide to Wicca
(with Paul Tuitean)
Crossing Press, 1998, Freedom, CA

Essential Wicca
(with Paul Tuitean)
Crossing Press, 2001, Freedom, CA

Color a Magick Spell
(with Anne Marie Forrester)
Self-published, Anne Marie Forrester, 2010

TAROT LORE

AND

OTHER B.S.

Estelle Daniels

Illustrations by
Peggy McDowell

Jester Studio Publishing

Published by Jester Studio Publishing
Tomahawk, WI 54487
(715) 453-9632

Cover design by Wimm/Jester Studio Publishing
Book design by Wimm/Jester Studio Publishing

First Printing 2014

ISBN-13: 978-0692317358
ISBN-10: 069231735X

DEDICATION

To the North Star Tarot Conference, Nancy and Melanie.
You guys rock!

And also to my Mother who has always encouraged and
supported me with my esoteric studies, be it astrology,
tarot or whatever. You rock, Mom!

TABLE OF CONTENTS

INTRODUCTION

This is a book about tarot cards. Not one that explains what each card is about, or how to do readings, but one about the lore and mystique that surrounds the cards and reading the cards and all the many thou shalt's and thou shalt not's surrounding the cards. There are a whole lot of do's and don'ts surrounding tarot, and much received lore that is passed along from book to book, teacher to student, and reader to reader.

Now, I have no special new or deep insights about the cards and their meanings. I don't have a bunch of new and exciting spreads. But I do have a finely tuned BS detector, and so that's what this book is about. They do say write about what you know... It's written in a hopefully humorous style. It's irreverent and bursts many balloons, or alternatively tips over the sacred cows—thereby mixing metaphors. If all the lore you've learned about the cards is **received sacred wisdom,** and you believe in it wholeheartedly, this book is not for you. If you enjoy tarot and are open to new ideas and some fun, then read away!

Trouble is, most of this received tarot lore is pure BS. What? The lore is BS? Yep, and that's what this book is about. Debunking myths. No holds barred. I get into the down-and-dirty of what it's really about, and maybe some real-world reasons for some of the lore, but there are many statements and some stuff that is pure BS, totally fabricated and pure crap. And I really mean it about the totally fabricated part. You'll know when we get there.

I have enjoyed, studied, read and collected tarot since the very early 1970's. I currently own way too many decks, work with a group that meets monthly, attend tarot conferences, speak about and teach tarot at festivals and in group settings. I'm also an astrologer, something which is a no-no in astrology circles (but that's another book...) but something which is somewhat common and appreciated in tarot circles. I have also written several other books, but you can find those listed on a previous page. This is my first book on the subject of tarot. I hope you'll enjoy it, or at least get a few laughs, and in these tense and hectic times a good laugh is usually greatly appreciated. And necessary.

In the early 1970's there were exactly four tarot decks available at major book stores (Kroch and Brentano's at Old Orchard—before it got big—to be precise). The Marseilles Tarot, the Swiss Tarot, the Rider Waite Tarot and the brand new Aquarian Tarot. And I was a young pup, looking for a deck to tell fortunes with. Even though I loved the faces on the new Aquarian Tarot, I chose the Rider Waite as the pips (numbered suit cards—Ace to 10) were pictorial. That is, the deck had an individual distinct picture for each and every card—pips included. The Aquarian Tarot had regular pips—i.e. cards depicting a number of the items of that suit only, no special pictures. I like special pictures.

I also bought a book to go with my new cards, The Tarot Revealed by Eden Gray. A good book, and the pictures matched my deck. Better.

So I read the book and worked with the cards, and read more and more widely (there was no internet in those ancient times) and came across an amazing amount of tarot lore—not about what the cards meant, or specific spreads to use for readings. No, there were an amazing number of do's and don'ts surrounding the cards: how to store them, how to use them, what you should never do, and so on and so forth. Being young and impressionable,

I dutifully followed all those 'rules', or at least the ones I knew about. I wrapped my deck in a silk scarf when I was not using it. I read for myself and my friends. I used the 'approved' reading spreads and all that.

A young girl's fancy turns to cards

Well, I'm older now, and much less naive and impressionable. And I've also read a LOT more widely and thoroughly. Some of it even on the internet, now that it exists. And in all that, I've discovered that many of these rules are mutually exclusive, restrictive and just plain dumb. So here is my take on all this lore, what the real deal is, and where this BS might have originated.

1 TAROT: WHAT IT IS

For those not familiar with tarot cards (and what rock have you been living under to know nothing about tarot cards?), I will describe them briefly.

Tarot is a deck of cards, traditionally 78 in number. 56 of them are the suit cards: 4 suits of 14 cards each. Each suit has 10 numbered cards, from Ace to 10—the pips, and four court cards: Page, Knight, Queen and King. The Page or Knight corresponds to the Jack in regular playing card decks. The other is an 'extra' card. The four traditional suits of tarot are Wands, Cups, Swords and Pentacles or Coins. They correspond to the suits of Clubs, Hearts, Spades and Diamonds in a regular playing card deck. These cards are also called the Minor Arcana. It sounds more important and magical.

The Major Arcana of the tarot deck

1

Then there's the 'extra' suit—the Trumps, AKA the Major Arcana—22 cards with distinct pictures, numbers and names. These are the ones that spook the uninitiated and fundamentalists. One is Death, for heaven's sake! Even if you know nothing else about tarot cards, you certainly know that if the Death card comes up, someone's gonna die! Well, duh! Yeah, people die every day. And people are born every day, but there's no 'birth' card in the deck, so that's not an issue. Get over it. We all will die eventually, so let's get on to the lore and the BS.

Backside of the Major Arcana

2 The True Received History of Tarot

The first tarot lore you may learn is about the Gypsies/Bohemians who originally came from India, and traveled to Egypt. These people were ancient and worldly-wise. They brought with them many secrets from the far East, and had much magic and wisdom of their own. Interestingly, nobody ever says why they left India in the first place and came to Egypt, just that they did. I think they missed a good story there, but hey, I'm just repeating what I've learned.

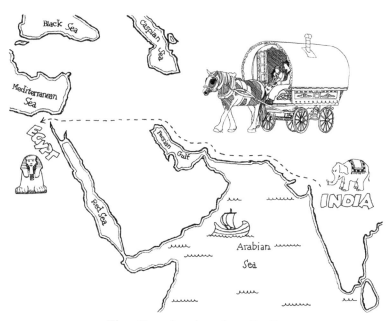

The Gypsies leaving India

And we're really lucky they did, because when the Gypsies arrived in Egypt, they ran into the last Priests of the Ancient Egyptian religion and magical tradition. Everybody knows Ancient Egypt was magic—just look at their writing and artifacts and it's immediately apparent. So these few ancient priests were hanging around, waiting to die, and despairing that their vast ancient secrets and magical knowledge would be lost forever, because they were the last ones. Did I mention there was nobody else available to carry on their traditions? Just making sure.

The last Egyptian priests

Then came the Gypsies. The Priests and the Gypsies immediately recognized in each other adepts of a secret and magical nature, and they got together, hung out, and traded lore, knowledge and the secrets of Life, the Universe and Everything. It was a good time. But all good times come to an end. The Gypsies were a nomadic race. They could never stay in any one place for any great time. Or at least never settle permanently anywhere.

So the Gypsies learned what they could from the Ancient Egyptian Priests, added it to their own considerable lore, and moved on to Europe.

What exactly was this Ancient Egyptian lore? It was, of course, everything about the Ancient Egyptian civilization, their Gods, magic and other stuff, but also the knowledge of other ancient sages: Moses and the Hebrews (remember Moses and Co. did a considerable stint in Egypt), Hermes Trismegistus, Alchemy, the Templars, maybe some goodies from the Arabic and Persian civilizations and certainly any other magical stuff that was hanging around at the time.

The Egyptian priests and Gypsies together

The sages talk of magical golden tablets, set into the walls of the Egyptian Priests' temples. 22 or 78 tablets (the reports vary) of pure gold, inscribed with special pictures containing symbols so magical and ancient that they are forbidden to any but the most rigorously trained adepts. Anyone else looking upon them without the proper training would be struck dumb/blind/mad/ insensible/whatever. These are the basis of the tarot cards—this is where the pictures came from. And in these illustrations are contained all the knowledge of the world. So they were really special.

But they don't exist anymore because when the last of the priests died the pictures went away. Or were melted down for plate. Or were stolen. Or were destroyed by the ignorant and uninitiated masses. Or whatever. They are gone, you can't see them, no matter where you look. Unless they finally open that secret room inside/under the sphinx that contains all the knowledge of Ancient Egypt. More lore, but for another book...

The Egyptian temple with golden tablets

But the Gypsies were allowed to copy these magical images, and carry those copies with them as part of their mission to preserve all the esoteric lore of the world. So they did.

Exactly what time did all this take place, you ask? Well, that varies according to who is telling the story. It could be as early as 'ancient times'. You figure out when that may be, because those authors are strangely silent on actual dates. Then some others say the 1100's, the 1200's, the 1300's and so forth. Certainly the 1300's is the latest all this could have happened.

Anyhow, what happened next varies. The authors who advocate 'ancient times' for all of this, have the Gypsies with their magical stuff and all the Ancient Egyptian stuff, (plus Moses, Hebrews, Hermes Trismegistus, etc. etc.) arrive in ancient Rome. Again, at exactly what date is never is revealed. But dates notwithstanding, the Gypsies were there for a while, and they added to their already considerable lore that of Rome and Ancient Greece (The Greeks had brought all their best stuff to Rome anyhow). You could learn almost anything in Rome, and so they rounded out their magical and esoteric education there.

The Gypsies arriving in Rome

So to be complete, we have the Gypsies' original magic and lore from India, whatever they picked up on the way to Egypt, the stuff they got from the Ancient Egyptian Priests, plus the stuff from Moses and the Hebrews (does that sound like a rock group or what?), Alchemy, Persian and the Arabic civilizations, Ancient Rome, Ancient Greece, and anything else we might have overlooked. They had it all! Remember, Gypsies are inherently magical—they are from India you know, and India is also magical. So all their magic naturally attracted all the other magic that *was hanging around the ancient world because the ancient world was lots more magical than the modern times are.*

Their stint in Rome is not mentioned by other authors. The other authors have the Gypsies moving directly from Egypt to 'Europe'. What route they took, or how they got there is also not mentioned. But the next thing all the authors agree upon is that the Gypsies landed in France, coming in through the region of Bohemia. That's why they are called Bohemians. They ended up in France, and brought all their magical knowledge and lore to the world.

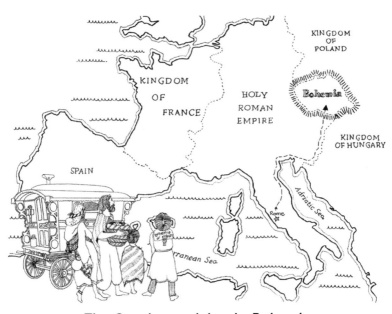

The Gypsies arriving in Bohemia

Like Europe is the world. Well it was, in those days. Nothing was happening anywhere else. Europe was the center of it all. Just ask those Europeans of the time—they certainly didn't know much of anything about anywhere else...

So somewhere in the travels between Egypt and France, the

Gypsies had changed the pictures on those golden tablets in the Ancient Egyptian Priests' Temples into a deck of cards. And not only that, but they also made up a game to go with these cards. The rationale was that they would put all these secrets of Life, the Universe and Everything on these cards. People would play the card game, and not really understand that they contained all this magical and esoteric knowledge of Life, the Universe and Everything. But because it was a simple card game, and people always like games, the knowledge would continue to be passed down the ages, unwittingly passed along from deck to deck. Pretty clever, huh?

Everyone playing the tarot card game

Now what happened to the part where people couldn't look on these images without proper magical understanding and not be struck dumb/blind/mad/insensible/whatever, and having them on playing cards that everyone looked at, but didn't understand their incredible secrets? Nobody talks about that part... Maybe the translation from gold to paper made them less damaging to the ordinary mortal. Insert your best guess here. That's mine.

Supposedly the first 'modern' western tarot deck was painted by an artist, Jacquemin Gringonneur, in 1392, 17 cards of which survive in the Bibliotheque National in Paris, for King Charles VI (or IV or VII—but it was King Charles anyhow) of France.

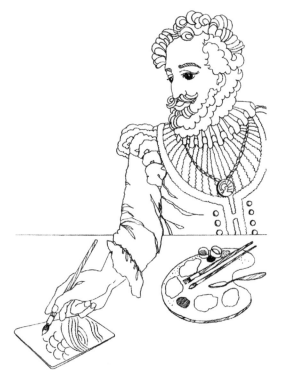

Jacquemin painting a tarot card

The Gypsies had allowed him to copy their cards, and he made fancy copies for his noble patron. The masses played games with tarot, while the intelligentsia understood the cards for what they *were and used the esoteric knowledge to expand their understanding of Life, the Universe, and Everything. It was the beginnings of Modern Western Occultism.* Wow! That's deep! (Oh yeah, it's getting really deep here...)

So this game of tarot, variously also known as tarocchi, triompfi, triumphs, tarok, trumps and other names, spread throughout Europe (the world!). *People everywhere (most everywhere) played the game, kept printing decks, and thereby spread all that sacred, secret and esoteric magical lore around for any adept to divine. What a clever plan. But then we all know Gypsies are clever and tricky. And magical, too.*

Court de Gébelin divining a card

Antoine Court de Gébelin was supposedly struck a few years before 1776 with the revelation that the Trumps—Major

Arcana—came from Egypt (there was widespread Egyptmania at the time), at a salon in Paris where some ladies were playing tarot. The hostess had recently traveled to Germany and Switzerland, where the game was still played (it having gone out of fashion in France some decades before) and brought the game back to Paris as a novelty for her guests. He spied The World card, and proceeded to give the esoteric meaning of the card. Then when the excited players presented him with the other trumps one by one, he soon divined their 'original' Egyptian origins and meanings. He was one of those adepts who could understand the esoteric meanings of the cards, being an enlightened person.

From Etteilla we learn that the Book of Thoth—generally meant to refer to the 22 Major Arcana—was devised by a committee of 17 Magi, presided over by Hermes Trismegistus in the 171st year after the Flood—3953 years before he recorded the fact in 1783. (Remember, this is predicated on the idea that the universe is 6000 or so years old.)

The committee of Magi discussing the Major Arcana

Eliphas Levi said 'an imprisoned person, with no other book than the Tarot, if he knew how to use it, could in a few years

acquire universal knowledge'. Eliphas Levi is the Father of West-
ern Occultism, so whatever he said has to be true. He certainly
wrote a lot of important stuff, some of it on tarot.

Papus called the tarot the absolute key to occult science. Tarot
cards are magical and special and contain all the important
knowledge and occult stuff any person could want. Nothing else
is needed. Papus wrote the definitive history of the tarot—<u>The</u>
<u>Tarot of the Bohemians</u> *(still in print—Dover). His accounts*
gathered together all the extant lore, and published it in one
convenient volume. He knew it all, and shared it with the world.

Thus runs the received history and lore of Tarot.

Pretty heavy stuff, right?

WRONG! This history mostly comes from Papus' <u>Tarot of</u>
<u>the Bohemians</u>—who stole some of it from Antoine Court
de Gébelin, made the rest up, and is pure BS. And Papus'
original tale has been embellished and added to and elaborated upon through the decades since he wrote it. Really.
But it is a nice book, and the only one widely circulated
on the subject before the 1990's, so everyone believed it.
After all, if it's in a book, it has to be true, right? Sigh. Not
necessarily...

Playing cards came from China, through India, through
the Islamic world in the 1100's or so, and then on to Europe
with the paper craft and trade in the 1300's. These cards are
similar to our standard 52 card deck: 4 suits and 13 cards
per suit—3 court cards and 10 pips per suit.

The Tarot part—the Major Arcana or Trumps—were
'pasted' on to a variant of this 'standard deck' during the
Italian Renaissance in Northern Italy (for sure by 1425 or
so) as an invention for game playing as permanent trumps—
making triompfi a trump card game, and centuries later
the deck became a vehicle for fortune telling.

The extra court cards were inserted into the standard 52 card deck some time in the 1300's— the Queens, probably in France.

Someone secretly inserting the extra queens

The Gypsies were actually nomadic tribes moving into Europe in the early 1400's from their origins in India. They call themselves the Rom or Roma. Their popular name 'Gypsies' came from a misunderstanding of their origins in Egypt. The French called them Bohemians because that was the region from which they first entered France, and spread from there. That part, at least, was true. One sentence in all that. Think about it.

There is no proof anywhere of Gypsies reading fortunes

with cards—tarot or otherwise—until the early 1900's. Oops.

Less romantic, more plausible. So I've just burst a whole lot of bubbles here, and I leave you a field of tipped-over sacred cows.

A field of tipped-over sacred cows

And until the 1990's all this 'received' lore was considered THE TRUTH about the origins of tarot. In the 1990's scholars and historians looked into the real origins of playing cards, tarot cards, the occult use of tarot cards and so forth. And lo and behold, they discovered all the old history was crap. Did you notice that part about Papus stealing some and making up the history in his magnum opus, <u>Tarot of the Bohemians</u>? Yeah. That's the sort of sterling research most of these earlier authors used. They made it up. Wholesale. Some called it revealed or channeled knowledge. Everyone knows Gypsies are magic, and tarot cards are magic, so the Gypsies brought the tarot cards to Europe from Egypt, because the Gypsies came from Egypt. Good reasoning that.

3 MORE ALTERNATIVE TAROT HISTORIES

Tarot was not created by the Ancient Egyptian Priests—they inherited tarot from the vast store of knowledge brought to Ancient Egypt after the fall of Atlantis. This makes the tarot way older than even Papus imagined. Everyone knows the Atlanteans were really smart and very magical so it just stands to reason they invented the tarot and brought it to ancient Egypt where their Priests kept and passed on that important knowledge to the present day. This is a more modern version of the Gypsies from India history—they just paste on Atlantis at the start, and have the Gypsies still doing their thing with the Ancient Egyptian Priests. Atlantis shows up in the history of tarot mostly in the 20th century. Probably an Age of Aquarius thing.

Perhaps tarot came from Atlantis

Paul Foster Case, a prominent esotericist in the U.S., did not necessarily believe in the Gypsies from India version of the history of tarot. He did comment on the various somewhat contradictory accounts extant in the 1920's that one could read about. He instead concocted his own version of the 'true history of tarot'. Case was a Mason and also believed that the Brotherhood of the Rosy Cross (supposedly founded by Christian Rosenkreutz in the 1300's) was real and helped preserve secret ancient traditions—among them being tarot. So his history takes all this into account.

Scholars in Fez in Morocco invented tarot in the 12th century. Whether there was a specific group of people who got together and came up with the tarot, or whether it was the product of one person, or a school of thought is not detailed.

As time has gone on, this tale has been elaborated upon and embellished by others. Now it's more fully fleshed out.

In the 12th century in the city of Fez in Morocco there were many schools of religious, esoteric and scholarly subjects. The Jews had their schools, and were busy formulating the Kabbalah there. Others had schools of esoteric learning, and in this atmosphere, the tarot was invented—an amalgam of esoteric and Kabbalistic thought refined into a deck of 78 cards, with the 22 trumps having the highest esoteric and Kabbalistic importance. From Fez, these cards, in the form of a simple card game, traveled to Italy with sailors who brought the pastime with them on their voyages. Once the cards 'landed' in Italy, they spread across Europe.

In the late Middle Ages, much learning and mystical lore was prominent in various Arabic cultures, and spread with the conquests of Islam. Fez in Morocco was one center of learning and scholarship in the 12th century. There was a Jewish 'colony' there, and Kabbalah was being formulated before, during and after that time, in various places by various Jewish groups. And the Arabic cultures saved and elaborated on much mystical and occult lore after the fall of Rome. With the spread of Islam, these schools of learning followed and many centers of learning under the aegis of various Islamic rulers sprang up all around the Islamic world, which included Fez in Morocco. But there is absolutely no proof anywhere that tarot was extant in Morocco before modern times.

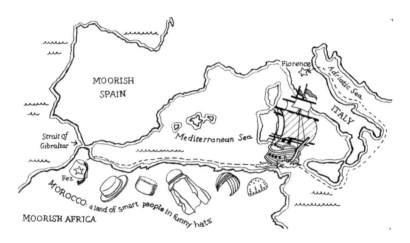

Land of smart people with many different hats

So Paul Foster Case was also subject to the same disease Papus fell to—he made it up. True, he felt he had some reason for advocating this particular history—Masonic lore and all that—but in the end, it was still created out of whole cloth, with the same sterling research used by Papus and company.

Eugene Caslant mentions in a book introduction that the Greeks could have carried the original Tarot from Ancient Egypt to Marseilles. This cuts the Gypsies from India out of it totally, but preserves the Ancient Egyptian Priests, etc. Now why the Greeks would have been running around the Mediterranean with tarot cards, and not the Romans or whoever is not mentioned. Caslant makes the mistake of thinking that Marseilles is the 'origin' of Tarot in Europe because of the prevalence of the Marseilles Tarot. Unfortunately Marseilles was only a 'center' of Tarot from the 1700's onward, which is much later than the true 'origin' of Tarot, no matter which history you subscribe to.

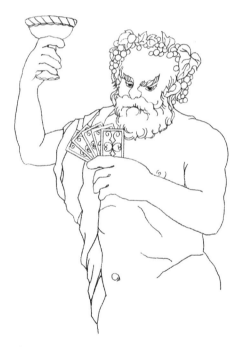

Dionysus contemplates his cards

Paul Huson also involves the Greeks. He read in Leland's book, <u>Aradia, or the Gospel of the Witches,</u> that there was an incantation where the Goddess Laverna is summoned by spreading 40 cards, symbolic of 'superior gods'. *Huson felt these 40 cards were the same as the 40 trumps found in the Minchiate/Florentine Tarot. He then goes further to suggest these triumphi—an older name for tarot—might preserve the mysteries of the God Dionysus. The name triumphi was a derivation of the Greek word thriambos, which was a precessional hymn in honor of Dionysus. Huson felt the tarot preserved many Pagan themes from this Greek Dionysian origin.*

Once again, an author takes a tentative correlation and turns it into a 'true' history. Just because two words are similar does not mean they have the same origins. And just because some tarot decks have Jupiter and Juno, instead of the Pope and Popess, does not make the deck of Greek Dionysian origin. More sterling research.

Manly P. Hall was skeptical of the 'Gypsies from India' history of Tarot. He presents many other versions, but the first and most elaborate brings in a different thread of Masonic lore. *The Tarot was brought to Europe by the Knights Templar who discovered their lore and wisdom while they were helping pilgrims in the Middle East during the crusades. They were learned in esoteric and occult lore, recognized important stuff when they saw it, and brought the cards back with them when they left the Holy Land after it was reconquered by the Muslims. They spread the decks throughout Europe, and disguised their esoteric significance by making them into a deck of cards for playing mundane games.*

Hall was a Mason, and his magnum Opus, <u>The Secret Teachings of All Ages</u> is a paean to Masonic esoteric lore and learning. To his credit, he remains somewhat skeptical of all the various histories, but he really lays it on about the Templars, and that coincides with Masonic history and lore, so that's the one the reader assumes he subscribes to.

The Knights Templar and their treasure

Unfortunately, little concrete evidence exists about exactly where the Templars got all their money (they arrived as paupers in the Holy Land, and returned centuries later fabulously wealthy), let alone what esoteric or magical lore they collected. If anything.

Most of the bad press about the Templars was made up by their detractors, people who owed them money and thereby conspired with the Pope to have them shut down, their estates confiscated, and the leaders tortured and burned at the stake. This was Friday, October 13th 1307, in France, and is the origin of the legend of Friday the 13th being unlucky. It certainly was for the Templars! There is nothing to indicate tarot cards, playing cards or anything like that came back with the Templars. Only that vast fortune they 'found' while in the Holy Land, and scholars and archaeologists are still having fistfights over that one.

You can watch many of them on the History Channel and similar vehicles.

The most contemporary origin of Tarot comes from a person who was supposedly there at the time and witnessed it!

The Tarot was brought to Earth by the Space Brothers in 1978 to a backyard in Berkeley California. Supposedly a barbecue was in progress, and they showed up, invited themselves in and had a good time. They were looking to hang out with Elvis, and left tarot cards as a 'thank you' for the hospitality, even though they didn't meet Elvis. The Space Brothers were aliens, though in disguise.

The Grays handing the tarot to the Hippies

This is amazing, as we have an eyewitness here. On the other hand, it flatly contradicts the many, many references we have to Tarot in many places from the 1400's to 1977—including this author who bought her first tarot deck around 1970, which was definitely before 1978. Of course aliens have perfect control of space, time and matter, so even though they originally brought tarot to Earth in 1978, they can retroactively make them 'appear' in many times and places from the 1400's to 1977 in a massive retro-re-writing of history and the development of mankind.

Whether the aliens were the grays or blacks, is not recorded. I suspect the grays as they are the 'good' aliens. And they are cuter, and we all know cute is an important element of tarot. Well, at least in some derivational tarot decks, cute is highly important.

So if you believe in aliens, this history of tarot is for you. For the rest of us, it sounds like a bad acid trip. Which was definitely going around in Berkeley in 1978, eyewitness or not.

So now that I've debunked the various received histories of the tarot, I'll go on to the rest of the lore.

The Grays go home

4 Tarot Lore: The Basics

Most of the lore consists of a series of do's and don'ts. There are many statements about what is okay and not okay to do, and what is and isn't legitimate about tarot. And there's a lot of it. Now, in all this do and don't stuff, there's never really much about reasons or consequences for breaking the sacred received rules. Well, in the interest of completeness, I have made a study of this all, and I know what will happen if you don't do stuff right.

Ready? It's pretty dire.

Warning—this coming paragraph isn't for the faint of heart.

You've been warned.

Okay, you forced me...

I'll tell you.

Everyone knows tarot cards are magic, right? Well if you do things wrong, the consequence is that the magic leaks out of your cards—sometimes pretty dramatically. And non-magical tarot cards won't work. At all. You might as well use a plain old playing card deck, as use a non-magical tarot deck. There are ways to recharge a deck—keep reading. But better to keep the original magic in the deck, than to have to recharge it.

And occasionally, I've heard that some forbidden practices can cause a deck to explode. Really. The psychic energies get so awfully and profanely screwed up, that the deck explodes and sometimes takes out anyone within six feet of them. Or render the cards' owner dumb/blind/mad/insensible/whatever. It's really ugly, this tarot card explosion. And it psychically scars everyone and everything within radius of the blast. And sometimes even starts a fire.

It's a bad thing. So you'd better follow the rules, or it will turn out badly. You have been warned.

Magical and non-magical tarot decks

Alternatively, the Tarot Police™ will come and take your deck away. Maybe even brand you psychically as a failed tarot reader—someone who profanes the rules and doesn't deserve to be allowed to study and read tarot anymore. You had your chance, and you blew it by breaking the rules. Now, I've never seen the Tarot Police™ myself, but my sister's friend's cousin heard about a guy who was visited by them and it was a big deal and he was psychically scarred for the rest of his life! It was really bad.

I'm an expert in all of this, and know all about it. My

sterling research on the above paragraphs is the same as Papus, and Etteilla and Court de Gébelin, and maybe even Eliphas Levi. Think about it. You'll figure it out eventually.

Tarot Policeman™

5 CARE AND STORING OF YOUR TAROT DECK

Now that we've taken a look at the history and some of the lore surrounding tarot we can discuss the care and treatment of your deck.

Tips for caring for your deck from a prominent esoteric author:

◊ Wrap your deck in a protective cloth
◊ Store your deck in a box embellished with protective and/or empowering symbols
◊ Before reading, cleanse your deck of negative energy by putting all the cards back in order and upright. You can also smudge the cards with sage or any other cleansing incense or herb.
◊ Wrap stones or crystals with your deck, or put them on top of the deck box. Select stones or crystals with healing or protective properties or ones that absorb negative energy.
◊ Place your deck on the windowsill in the light of the full moon.

You must keep your deck wrapped in a silk cloth. This is the first lore most any tarot student learns. Supposedly, this is to help keep the magic in your cards. Now we all know that tarot is magical, and the pictures contain all the received wisdom of the ancient world...

Oops, sorry about that. That stuff is so romantic and esoteric and neat, I forget sometimes. We do know tarot cards are magical because we just do. Look at them—how can they be anything except magical? And silk is insulating and also magical. Well, all the magical traditions (or those that use robes) tell their initiates that they must wear magical robes, made of natural fibers, preferably silk. So if it's good enough for magical rituals, it should be good enough for tarot cards, too. Anyway, silk is a good insulator. So maybe wrapping your cards in silk will help insulate them from the vibes of the world at large. That's the best rationale I can figure for this one. Take it or leave it. Alternatively, people who sell silk cloths may be behind this one.

You must keep your deck wrapped in a cloth of silk, or cotton. You must never use wool or leather as using animal products will dull the magic in the cards. Yeah, no animal products here! (Are tarot cards vegan?) Except silk is made from the cocoons of silkworms. They are insects, but insects are alive and no self-respecting vegan would ever eat a silkworm or any other insect. And what about linen, which is also made from plant materials—flax to be precise. Makes a person wonder about what else they may have left out.

Your deck must be stored in a drawstring bag, specially made for Tarot cards. The bag can be made of silk, or possibly lined with silk. Velvet or other fabrics are possibly okay, too. At least I have seen bags made from velvet and other fabrics, so they must be okay, because they were for sale in a Metaphysical shop, and everything in that sort of shop is magic and they would never sell something that was not okay or bad or cause problems...

Anyone ever hear the phrase 'caveat emptor'? That's Latin for 'let the buyer beware'. It applies to Metaphysical shops, too. Sorry shopkeepers.

The bag must have French seams—fully finished seams—no raw edges anywhere, and not contain any zippers or buttons. The French seams rule might be because raw seams could cause wear and tear on the cards, but I think it's because someone made bags with French seams and they wanted to make sure people would only buy their bags, and so they said all other bags were bad or wrong. Alternatively, raw seams are like little electrical brushes and they leach the magic out of the cards, rendering them useless. Can you see the little metaphysical sparks as the cards rub against the raw seams? You can't? More about that later...

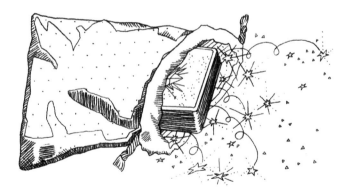

Tarot deck in an inappropriate bag

Buttons and zippers are just wrong. A zipper is way too modern (invented in 1909—more useless trivia at no extra cost!) and modern stuff can't be magical so a zipper will allow the magic to leak out of the cards. Especially a plastic zipper. As to buttons—well buttons (which date from pre-historic times) are lots older than zippers, but someone said buttons are wrong, so they must know and so that's that. More sterling research and/or reasoning.

One thing they don't talk about is the cards wrapped in silk, and then put into a bag. This is the belt and suspenders theory. Or are they put loose in the bag, without the silk cloth? Inquiring minds want to know.

Your deck must be stored in a special box—preferably wood—some say it must be hand-made—and sometimes embellished with psychic, magical and/or protective symbols. One presumes the deck is stored in the box, wrapped in the silk cloth.

The box housing your tarot deck should be made of pine. If not pine, oak is OK, but never yew, maple or any fruitwood. Pine is easily obtained and worked. Oak is tougher to work, but it holds up well over the centuries. Yew is the death wood, and putting the Death card in the death wood, Brrrr. Creepy. Forget about it. Maple is very hard and difficult to work. Fruitwoods, I don't know. I do know a recorder made from fruitwood is supposed to sound sweeter. What that has to do with tarot cards...

So what's this special box thing about? Nowadays, it's mostly promulgated by the people who make and sell special boxes for tarot decks. Caveat emptor again.

There is a plausible older reason for the wooden box, however. Really. Back 200+ years ago, in most people's houses (yes, even the rich/fancy ones) bugs, mice and rats were a continual problem. That's one reason many people kept dogs and cats. They chase and eat bugs, mice and rats. But they can't catch all of them, and paper is a favorite food and nesting material for vermin. So that pretty deck, made of paper that you left on the shelf might get nibbled away if you don't store it in a sturdy box, where the vermin can't get in. This is a real practical reason for the box. The symbols are probably optional, as I think the box will be as useful protecting the cards from vermin with or without the symbols.

Mice feasting on an unprotected deck

The lore is silent on metal or stone boxes. Might be interesting to check this one out. Alternatively, maybe not. Don't want the Tarot Police™ knocking on my door, threatening to take away all my tarot decks. The Tarot Police™ are real! Someone mentioned them once in a blog I read a couple years ago...

A plastic box is bad, and cards should never be stored in a plastic box—it cuts them off from psychic vibrations and nullifies the magic. Really. Everyone knows you can't wear or use plastic in magical ceremonies, enchantments or spells—dit nullifies the magic. Really. I read that in a book about magic and everything in books is true, right? And plastic is modern and modern stuff can't be magic, only old stuff.

Also plastic is made from petroleum products, and you'd never put your deck in oil, but using a plastic box is just the same. So everyone agrees, plastic is a bad thing, and keep it away from your tarot cards, period.

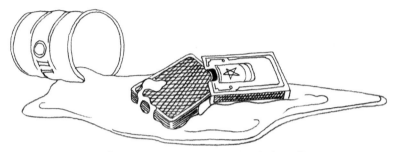

You'd never put your deck in oil...

But the cards themselves are coated in plastic... Huh? Yep, most all cards—playing and tarot—are coated in plastic. That's what makes them more shiny, more sturdy and somewhat waterproof and pliable so they can be shuffled without creasing. So how do we reconcile the 'no plastic' rule with this reality? We don't. Sometimes it's easier to close your eyes to reality than to admit a rule of received lore is stupid and/or wrong. Alternatively, check out my theory of how the magic gets into the cards, and anything done to the cards beforehand doesn't count. Keep reading, you'll get to it.

So would a bag made of polyester, nylon or other similar man-made fabric be like storing your deck in a plastic box? Or is it a solid plastic box that makes it bad versus a pliable fabric bag? After all, there are small holes between the fibers in a fabric and maybe that allows the deck to breathe and allows the magic to be intact. And what about plastic wrap? The mind boggles at the implications! Hey, I'm playing with semantics here. Indulge me. After all, I'm debunking the lore and so I get to make stuff up, just like many of the people who started the lore did. More sterling research.

Additionally, all this scarf, bag, box stuff protects the cards from harmful sunlight. I know sun can bleach colors in clothes, so I guess it can harm paper as well. Of course, if you're leaving your cards out in the sunlight, they are also vulnerable to wind and rain and the rest of the elements. Or kids and pets and other people who don't respect the magical lore of tarot and might hurt the cards. The moral is, don't leave your cards out where they can get damaged. It's not rocket science.

Your tarot deck must be stored on a shelf, shoulder height or higher, near an egress. Egress? What's an egress?

P.T. Barnum had fantastic shows of wonders from all over the world. (Don't worry, I'll get to it.) Unfortunately these museum shows were so wondrous that people would stay and marvel for longer than he wanted them to. It was all about traffic, and having as many people per hour going through his 'museum' as possible, and paying for the privilege. More people going through faster = more money. Simple equation. So he got an inspiration. He had an elaborate sign painted, and placed it prominently in the last room with a convenient arrow. It read 'This Way to the Great Egress'.

People would look at the sign, and then get excited that something more was waiting, so they moved along briskly and he was able to get more people per hour into his museum, and thereby increase profits. Egress is Latin for exit. It worked for him and everyone knows P.T. Barnum was a great entrepreneur. More useless trivia for you to enjoy—my brain is full of it. (Oh yeah, you're full of it all right...)

P.T. Barnum's inspiration

Ahem. Stored on a shelf shoulder height or higher. Let's break this down. Whose shoulder? I'm roughly 5'6" or so. So is a shelf 5'2" high appropriate for me? What about someone who is over 6' tall. Or 7' tall? (Not many tarot readers in the pro basketball community, though.) Does their shelf have to be higher? What about a child, and what do you do as they grow? Do you move the shelf up each year? What if I'm wearing bitchin' 4 inch high heels? So this whole shelf thing is somewhat suspect.

This shoulder height shelf thing comes from the lore of care and use of the I Ching. I Ching is old, so that's OK, right? Old is magical and the I Ching is magical, too... Alternatively, there is a practical real-world reason for the shoulder-high shelf, and that is to protect your deck (or yarrow stalks— used originally for I Ching before someone devised the method using coins to save time) from flooding. Presumably if the flood is above shoulder height, the whole house would be gone anyhow, but a lesser flood would preserve the house, but ruin anything that ended up under water. So this bit of lore may be practical—at least for Ancient Chinese people.

Storing the cards near an egress—exit—may also have a practical reason. If your house catches fire, and you make your living reading cards like the Gypsies did... (Okay, I got carried away with the romance of Gypsy life again.) So your house catches fire, and you have to run to get out. If your cards are on a shelf near the door, you can grab them on the way out, and save your cards from the fire. Makes some sense. Alternatively, Orthodox Jews have the eastern wall of their house partially unfinished (usually behind a picture) in remembrance of the destruction of the second temple in Jerusalem. So if the cards are stored on an eastern wall, on a shelf shoulder height or higher and by an egress, you are doing a lot of things right. And the cards contain the wisdom of Moses and the Hebrews (again—a great name for a rock band), so that makes it doubly good.

Never store your cards on or near a TV. This is a more modern rule. At least since 1947. TV vibes (known as RF—radio frequencies—by professionals in the business) adversely affect the cards. Whether it leaches the magic out, or just screws it up isn't detailed. But I bet it's bad, otherwise they wouldn't make a rule about it.

Now there is no rule that I know of about computers, cell phones, wifi, DVD's, VCR's, tablets, smart phones, and all that new-fangled electronic stuff. But all that is modern, and modern is non-magical, so it has to be bad, therefore I'm telling the world: *keeping tarot cards in proximity to any* of this electronic stuff will pull the magic out of them, and if too many electronic doo-dads are near the cards, they just may blow up. You have been warned!

Tarot deck carelessly left on a television

6 Using Your Deck

When reading the cards, they must never touch the table or ground. Everyone knows if they touch the bare table or ground the magic will leak out. This is the flag rationale. You learned this one in scouts—the flag much never touch the ground. If it does, it must be retired and burned.

Well, this gives us a valid reason for the silk cloth. You spread the silk cloth out over the table/ground/whatever and place the cards on that. But where do you place the cards after you've unwrapped them but before you spread the cloth out? Or do you spread the cloth one-handed? Decisions, decisions. Better make the right one, or the Tarot Police™ will get you!

Actually, before modern times, tables weren't all that smooth or even clean, so you'd want to put your paper cards on something to keep the gravy stains or dirt from ruining the deck. Or giving the cards splinters. Those could hurt! This was in the days before all cards were coated with plastic. (The explanation is coming, I promise. Keep reading.) This protecting from the dirty table is where tablecloths came from. Now table coverings of various types are used so things look nicer and possibly are more elegant and snooty. Things change over time.

When you or the person you are reading for shuffles the cards, you must never riffle shuffle the cards. This is the standard bridge/poker/casino style of shuffling a deck. It's very bad, and if you do this, the magic will poof out of the deck. If you take a tarot deck and riffle shuffle the cards (I'm proposing this as a thought-experiment. Far be it for me to recommend anyone doing anything that's forbidden), and you look carefully, you can actually see the greenish-yellow cloud of magic poofing out of the cards at the point of the riffle shuffle. Really. I promise. What? You can't see the greenish-yellow cloud of magic poofing out of the cards? I'll address that case later. (That's two things you are watching out for. For those who are keeping track.)

Riffle shuffling with the magic poofing out

Riffle shuffling can be hard on the cards themselves. They can get bent and weak and wear faster. Except modern cards are made to be able to withstand moderate use. That's a benefit of the plastic coating. (Yes, it's still coming.)

You can shuffle your deck gently using several methods.

The pool or mix shuffle has you place all the cards face down on a large table and move them around in a swirling motion with both hands while concentrating on the question. When I was a kid this was called a mess, and mom said we shouldn't play with the cards that way, but now it's an approved tarot shuffling method. How times change.

The side shuffle has you hold the deck loosely in one hand the long way, and pull a group of cards out and mix them gently back in the rest of the deck. Repeat as necessary until the deck is thoroughly shuffled. This one sometimes results in bunches of cards on the floor, but it isn't a riffle shuffle and so it does preserve the magic in the deck.

The multiple cut shuffle has you cut the deck into three piles, and then cut each of those piles into three more piles. Then reassemble the nine piles at random, cut the deck in half, and reassemble the deck. Again repeat as often as necessary until the deck is shuffled. Less messy, but still takes forever to properly shuffle. I guess this is why the riffle shuffle was invented, but it's still not good for tarot cards, so forget about it. I mean it!

Before any reading, the tarot deck must be shuffled 13 times. Is this so the cards are properly shuffled? Or because 13 is a magical and creepy number and sounds so much better than 12 or 14? That's a lot of shuffling, for sure! And make sure none of those shuffles are riffle shuffles! Gotta keep the magic in your deck.

You must never play games with your tarot deck—it profanes the sacred use of the cards. Um, except they were originally designed for playing games—in both the lore and historical fact. So there's no way getting around this one. Except nobody plays Tarot anymore—except the French and they have tournaments and the rest. But this book is in English, so it's an okay rule. Yeah, that's it unless you are in France (or Quebec) and speaking French (or Quebecois) you can't play games with tarot cards. And nowadays the game of Tarot uses a special deck that isn't a tarot reading esoteric magical deck. Yeah, that's it. So you must never play games with your tarot deck or the magic will leak out, or the Tarot Police™ will come and get you for sure!

You must never mix decks or use more than one deck in a reading. That will result in mixed energies, a bad reading, or the decks could explode. And if you think it's bad when one tarot deck explodes, imagine how much worse it is if two decks explode. Think about it. It's a horrible thought. <<Shudder>>

Two tarot decks exploding

When you do a tarot reading, you must use the entire deck. If you leave cards out, you are leaving out possibilities and not giving the full reading you could. Maybe there's some important warning in those unused cards, and you will be responsible for not imparting that valuable information. And some of the magic in the cards will leach away, unused. So use all those cards!

When you do a tarot reading, you must never use the entire deck. If you don't leave cards out, you are limiting the possibilities and not allowing for chance in your reading. There have to be mysteries, and if you tell everything in the cards by using all of them, then you will be responsible for imparting information that was best left unsaid. And you will use up all the magic in the cards. So don't use all those cards!

Does anyone see the problem with the two above rules? Yeah, you can't do both. So which is it? Which rule do you follow? Aarrrggghhhh! The angst of it all!

Tarot cards are for divination only. Any other use is profaning the sacred original intent of the cards. Tarot is for divination only—using it for anything else is bad and wrong. For example as quarter significators, for meditation, collecting for art/curiosity, playing games etc. So all those people who buy tarot decks as collector's items and collect for the art are doing a bad thing. And the Tarot Police™ will come and get them for sure. Tarot cards are magic and all the world's magical and esoteric wisdom is contained in them, and collecting them or playing games with them profanes their sacredness. Here you are wasting the magic, and it's just wrong to waste.

Except that over 50% of all decks that are sold are sold to collectors as art, not for reading. Dan and Jeanette, the people at tarotgarden.com told me this—so it has to be true. They make their living selling tarot cards. They know.

Hmmm, how do we reconcile this one? I think the people who make and sell tarot cards would be against this rule, as it would result in fewer tarot decks being sold, therefore fewer decks would need to be made. And I collect decks, so this rule is just BS. Yeah, that's it. This rule is BS. I said so, and it's in a book, so it has to be true. Polishing that sterling research again.

If you use them for meditation, that's a gray area. Meditation can be magical, so I guess it might be okay. I haven't heard of anyone having bad things happen because they used the cards for meditation. And using cards as quarter significators or depicting the Wheel of the Year—well a couple decks have diagrams that illustrate that exact thing. And those decks are still for sale, and I haven't heard of anyone being arrested or blown up by those decks for using them in those ways, so I guess that's okay. Until a bad rumor gets around—then it will be just wrong. That darn rumor mill!

Ye Olde Rumor Mill

7 MORE LORE ABOUT YOUR DECK

When you first get your new deck home, you must open it, put it to rest on a clean table, and allow it to breathe. That way it can breathe out the original factory energy and breathe in your energies. This can attune it to you. Yeah. I would presume you would unwrap all the plastic, and throw it away, and the naked deck will do the breathing. I have never heard a deck breathe—even brand new ones. Am I missing something?

Your tarot deck must never be handled by anyone other than you and the person you are reading for. Other people touching the deck will add their vibes and spoil the reading. They may also leach the magic out, and the cards won't work anymore. And maybe if you keep other people away, there is less chance for heckling.

Your deck must remain untouched by others

You must sort the cards after each reading—returning them to their original order and all upright. This is the airplane takeoff and landing rule. This is to eliminate the vibes from the person you read for and reset the cards for the next use. And it eliminates any negative vibes they might pick up from the reading or for having them out of their silk wrapping/bag/box.

So the cards are so delicate that they have to be handled carefully and put back in order after each reading. That's lots of sorting and making sure nobody touches them inappropriately (no, not **that** type of inappropriate touch). Sigh. Really? Tarot cards are powerfully magical, so powerful that if you use them improperly they can explode, but they are so wimpy that if anyone unauthorized touches them, they could lose their magic. Powerful or wimpy? They can't be both.

You must tap your deck three times on the table before every reading to chase out all the negative vibes. So tapping 'shakes out' all the negative vibes, and cleanses your deck. Whether or not this deck has been sorted after the previous reading is not known.

This one has the cards being not so delicate, but you still have to tap them on the table to shake out all the negative vibes. Why the negative vibes are 'tapped out' and the good ones and the magic stay in the cards is not related. Maybe the magic and good vibes are inherently stronger than the bad vibes. Tapping, sorting etc. sure has you handling those cards a whole lot, way more than you do when doing readings. So do they wear out faster? Inquiring minds want to know!

You must never buy a used—i.e. non-new and pristine—tarot deck because all used decks have negative vibes. Brrr. That's just creepy. So all those used decks at garage sales or second-hand stores are inherently tainted and 'unclean'. <<Makes the sign against the evil eye at the thought of unclean tarot cards.>>

Okay, whatever floats your boat. Again, the people who make and sell new tarot decks have a strong vested interest in making sure used tarot cards are forbidden. Yes, used tarot decks can be worn, stained, incomplete (drat—hate that one!), beat up and possibly dirty. But tainted and 'unclean'? Really? That's okay. I'll just take your old used decks that you don't want anymore and I'll make sure they are disposed of in an appropriate manner... I collect tarot decks so maybe I can get a few new decks this way. And those I don't need for my collection, I can sell to second-hand stores... Like P.T. Barnum, I'm always looking out for a way to make a quick buck. (You bought the book, didn't you?)

Your tarot deck must be new and unhandled by others. No human hands except your own (and possibly your clients) must touch your deck. Okay, this is just absurd.

DIGRESSION #1

Have you ever wondered about how tarot cards are made? How do they get into your hands?

Tarot cards are designed and created by someone. Once they have made all 78 images, they take their images/ideas to a publisher and the publisher eventually has those images printed on card stock. They come out in big giant sheets—10 x 8 cards on one sheet—that's 80 cards at one crack. The sheets are then cut up into individual cards, the cards sorted into a deck, and sometimes the deck and the little book it comes with are wrapped in plastic. Then the deck (and little book - wrapped in plastic or not) is placed into a cardboard box and that box is wrapped in plastic, and then with other decks is put into a larger box and shipped to stores, where they are unpacked and put on a shelf so you can see them in the store, pick them up and buy them.

That's a lot of hands handling the cards before you pick them up off that shelf. Let's count them, shall we?

People drawing the cards, publishing people looking at those drawings as they decide whether or not to buy the deck and print it out for sale. People who handle the drawings during production. And what about the person that writes the book accompanying the deck? If another person writes the book, they have to handle the drawings to see them so they can write the book to reflect those particular images.

Then at the publishing house, a person renders those original drawings into card-sized images, may tweak them to add edges, margins, names, numbers, interpretations and all that other stuff. Then those rendered images are turned into plates, and those plates are used to print the cards.

The giant printed sheets are then coated in plastic so the cards will be long-wearing and more sturdy and somewhat waterproof. Those giant uncut card sheets, now coated in plastic are moved to the cutting machine. And once cut, they are moved to the collating machines. Or they are collated by hand (which I helped do for the Tarot of Physics—that was a fun evening!). Then the collated cards are either wrapped in plastic or not, and placed in a cardboard box. Or occasionally a bag. And if in a box, they are wrapped in plastic again.

Then the finished decks are packed in larger boxes, shipped to a distributor or bookstore. At the distributor or bookstore, someone unpacks the box, and handles the deck as it's either shipped to stores or placed on a shelf for sale.

And what about the clerk who will certainly touch the deck as they scan the price before you have actually bought it? And then may touch it yet again by putting it into a bag so you can carry it home and start telling fortunes with the new cards you just bought.

Clerk at store handling the deck

That's a whole lot of hands involved in getting that new pristine deck to you. So how can your brand-new tarot deck be unhandled by others so as to make sure the magic docsn't leak out?

I have a theory. My research for this theory is similar to that done by Papus and Etteilla. In the grand tradition of sterling research on tarot lore, I'm proclaiming it's all true. So there!

This is Estelle's theory as to how the magic gets into the cards. The theory that is mine. Are you ready for this? Eh hem! <u>My Theory</u>, by Estelle.

My Theory, by Estelle

Once the cards are printed, coated in plastic and cut into cards, they are collated into decks. At that time, and no other, before they are either wrapped in plastic or put into the cardboard box without being wrapped in plastic first—they are spritzed with magic. This spritz of magic sort of seals the inherent magic in the drawings into the deck itself. Then the cards are either wrapped in plastic to seal the spritz of magic into the cards OR put into the box and that box is wrapped in plastic.

Anyhow, with all that plastic wrap, it seals the spritz of magic in the deck—and this is the ONE TIME that having plastic in contact with the cards is good. It's like the spritz is put on the cards, and then they are wrapped and put away and left to mellow/age/ferment/whatever. So that spritz leaches into the cards and permeates the cards, and that's how the tarot cards become so very magical and special. They marinade in magic for however long they sit in the box before you buy them. Sometimes that can be a short time, sometimes that can be years.

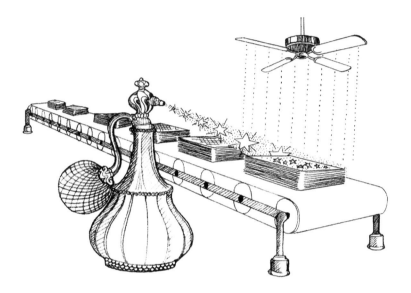

Decks being spritzed with Magic

But when people handle that sealed deck, it cannot affect the magic because the deck is sealed in the protective plastic, and the magic is safe and sealed away until you open that plastic, handle the cards, and put your special energy into the deck that is now yours forever.

Isn't that a wonderful theory? It's really elegant and explains a whole lot of things, while keeping that magic in the cards and away from people who would profane them. See, used decks have the plastic off them, so they have had their magic exposed to the world, and with all the people touching that deck—the person selling the cards, the clerk taking them in and valuing them, the clerk putting them on the shelf, the clerk handling them as you buy them and then bagging them—that's a lot of hands touching a poor unprotected deck. So you can totally understand how bad used tarot cards are. Brrrr. Creepy stuff.

(Bet you feel lots smarter after that. I know I sure do, and I wrote it.)

End of Digression #1.

Used tarot decks - creepy stuff

8 Yet More Lore About Your Deck

You must not buy your tarot deck. It must be a gift. I tried this one a lot with my mother. After I got my original Rider Waite deck, I read many tarot books and some showed other decks, and I had learned about this gift thing, and so I begged and begged to get some of those other decks. And mom's answer, 'maybe for Christmas or your birthday' wasn't really satisfactory. And I never got decks on those occasions anyhow. And no boyfriend was ever interested in giving me a deck, so that avenue was closed also.

Yeah, this one may come from some magical traditions where you must not buy your own athame (magical knife), it must be a gift. Or someone made it up. That has never happened before in the history of tarot lore. (Re-read that last sentence with a strong tone of snide sarcasm.)

You must never pay money for your deck, you must trade for the deck as using money will taint the magic in the cards. Except you trade the money for the cards... This is a filthy lucre rule. What is it about money that makes it so awful? Tell you what, you give me all your awful money/filthy lucre and I'll take care of it for you, and you will be untainted and pure. Just send it to me in envelopes of small denomination non-sequentially numbered bills. (P.T. Barnum, you got nothin' on me!)

When you purchase a deck of tarot cards, always receive it with your left hand. What is it about the left hand? And what if you are left handed—do you then use your right hand? Some people feel the left hand is the psychic, instinctual hand. And maybe that will help you be more in tune with the deck's magic. Except the magic isn't exposed until you unwrap the plastic. And are you buying it with money or barter? I'm confused. Do what you want.

If you get a deck, and you think it's icky, then really you are an icky person and maybe you shouldn't be reading tarot anyhow. All decks are magic, they are tarot decks, they have been spritzed with magic at the factory, they have mellowed in the box, and they were brought to the world (Europe) by the Gypsies from Egypt. So there can never be an icky deck. Ever.

I will personally dispute this statement. I have a lot of tarot decks (as well as other divinatory decks—more later) and there definitely are decks that are icky. Unfortunately you cannot get a consensus about icky decks.

Some people don't like Crowley's Thoth Tarot. Some swear by it and feel it's the most magical deck of all. Aleister Crowley—the self-styled wickedest man in the world—and Lady Frieda Harris collaborated on the deck in the 1930's and '40's. It was finally published in 1969, 22 years after Crowley's death. It was a true magical collaboration, and they purposefully designed it with magical intent. That makes it even more magical, if you buy into that stuff.

I have a deck I call the 'scribbly' deck—which is the 9th Dimension Tarot. It's old—late 1960's and the images look like they are derived from those pictures you do when you're a kid. You scribble on a piece of paper, and then look at the scribble and turn it into some sort of picture. Like a child's version of Rorschach tests. They are (to me) truly ugly and icky. Except the deck is old and rare, so icky or not, it's somewhat valuable, in terms of tarot cards. Sigh. I hate it, but never managed to get rid of it through the years, and now it's collectible so I keep it purposefully. But it's still icky to me.

So icky is as icky does. There's a theory that some people

are born to read tarot. Here's a story I learned from one of the many tarot books I read when I was younger.

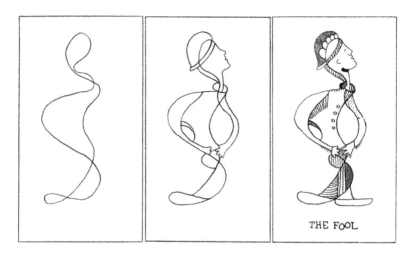

THE FOOL

Scribble is as scribble does

A Story About Tarot

A highly psychic young man was given a tarot deck. He had never seen one, but he immediately saw they were special and psychic and magical and he knew they were for divination. They came with a book, but he threw it away because once he looked at the cards, he intuitively knew their meanings and how to use them, and all the wisdom they contained. He naturally understood tarot and was able to give uncannily accurate readings from the start because he was a true psychic.

End of story.

And if your experience with tarot isn't similar, then you aren't really psychic enough to use them, and shouldn't have any. It will only damage you and profane the cards. *Only true natural psychics should ever read tarot,* and if you aren't you are a fake and a charlatan.

So stories notwithstanding, there is a school of thought that states you have to be psychic to read tarot, to even use or handle the cards in any way. Tarot readers are born, not made through classes, study or books. And if you're psychic, you can certainly see the magic leaking out when tarot cards are riffle shuffled, or put in a bag with raw edges. And if you can't see the magic leaking out, then you aren't psychic enough to be allowed to use tarot cards. It's a theory...

Believe what you will.

Magic glasses for the psychically impaired

9 YET STILL MORE TAROT LORE

Once you have been gifted/chosen a deck, that's it. That's your deck for all time. You are married to that particular deck for life. (Or longer if you buy into that stuff.) This is the monogamous tarot theory. Even variant sizes of the same deck are a no-no. Obviously this theory is not one the makers and sellers of new tarot decks will subscribe to, because then every reader will only get one deck, and that's it for life. They want to keep making and selling lots and lots of decks, so this one is a sales-killer.

Tarot reader being married to her deck

When you die, your tarot deck must be buried with you. This takes the *'married to one deck for life'* rule one step further. And what if you are cremated? Then there are people like me, who collect tarot decks and have many of them. If all my decks have to be buried (or cremated) with me, there would be no room in the coffin for me, because I have a lot of decks. Maybe I'll live forever because I can't be buried/cremated because there isn't a coffin big enough for all my decks and me also. Then again, living forever isn't fun unless you have eternal youth as well. And I'm a bit long in the tooth for eternal youth.

Another reason for this one is a rule that some of the magical orders have: when you die, your magical books are burnt and your magical tools are buried with you so nobody else can use them. Some people feel a tarot deck is a magical tool, and I do too. But buried with you? That coffin is getting awfully full.

Death with your decks

If you read tarot, you must only use one deck. You must never switch off decks. This is a corollary of the 'married for life' rule. Some maintain you can have one deck you use for readings for yourself, and another you use for readings for other people. And maybe another for study and meditation, and maybe yet another... Anyhow the question is, can you have only one deck, or can you have more than one deck? Makers and sellers of tarot decks want people to have as many decks as possible, so they can keep making and selling same.

The above two rules seem to want to restrict the number of decks any one person can have and/or read with. Why this would be, I cannot understand. It's probably old, because nowadays there are literally hundreds of decks to choose from, and it's just cruel to expect a person to stay with only one deck for life, when new and wonderful decks are coming out all the time. When there were 4 decks to choose from, this one might have made more sense. Then again, it's still a stupid rule.

If you lose or damage your deck, or one of the cards goes missing, or anything happens to your deck that makes it unfit for reading, then you are doing something wrong and you shouldn't be working with tarot at all. This is a corollary of your mother's saying 'take care of your things or you'll lose them'. Yeah. I guess this is another of those 'wimpy cards' rules. They are so fragile that if wear and tear happens, they will lose all their magic and not work anymore. This one supposes you are single, live alone, have no children or others that may find your cards and play with them while eating a PBJ sandwich. Or rip them up. Or bring them to class for show and tell. Or pets who might chew them or puke or pee on them. Anyhow, bad things happen, even to tarot decks. Cards can be replaced, trust me.

Time was, there used to be two blank cards in every deck. These were because a standard tarot deck has 78 cards, and cards are printed on large sheets in 8x10 groups. 8 X 10 = 80. 80 – 78 = 2. Two extra cards per deck—and they used to be blank. I was originally told this was so if you lost or damaged a card, you could replace it with one of those blank cards. Nowadays, those cards are printed with advertising and other important stuff the publisher wants you to read, so they're not as easy to make replacements from. Sigh.

Another Tarot Story

I was at the International Tarot Convention in May 2002 in Chicago, and there was a dinner and costume show. Many people wore colorful costumes and such to the dinner, but there were also these two guys and everyone wondered about them. They attended the dinner and walked around wearing white t-shirts, white boxers, white socks and athletic shoes and had white hotel towels hanging front and back pinned at their shoulders. They really stood out as looking pretty strange in the colorful elegantly costumed and dressed-up crowd.

Time came for the costume contest, and surprisingly, these two guys registered as part of it. Their turn came, and they walked onto the stage. They stood for a moment, turned around slowly and then said, "we're the two blank cards included in every deck." The audience was momentarily stunned, and then they got a standing ovation and eventually won a prize. When questioned afterward, they

said they didn't know about the costume contest beforehand, but once on site they wanted to participate, and after
brainstorming, this is what they came up with. Just goes
to show there's endless creativity in the tarot community
    End of story. Back to more lore.

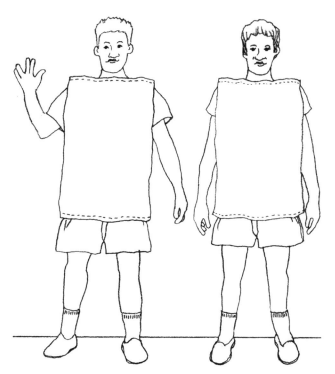

The two blank cards in every deck

10 AND YET STILL MORE LORE

C'mon—I'm full of it! (oh yeah, you are!) Well, at least enough for a book.

Take note of a few things the Tarot Police™ will surely be watching for.

◊ *Only you should ever handle your tarot deck.* Anyone else touching the deck will cause the magic to leak out.

◊ *Only the person you are reading for should touch your tarot deck,* because anyone else touching the deck will add extra energies and pollute the reading.

◊ *Only you and the person you're reading for should ever touch your tarot deck* as anyone else touching the cards will add extra energies and pollute the reading. Or all the magic will leak out. Or the Tarot Police™ will come and arrest you all.

(Anyone see the problem with these three rules? Yep. Mutually exclusive. Only you, only the person you are reading for, or both you and the person you are reading for but nobody else. Again I wonder, are the cards powerfully magical or so delicate and wimpy that most anything will disrupt their magic? Some people would have it both ways, no matter what.)

◊   A *tarot reading should only be done during the full moon.*
    So does that mean you can only read tarot cards
    at night? Or is the day of the full moon okay? (And
    don't get me started on that because as an astrol-
    oger I have different rules about it than others
    might...) Do you have to be outside? In winter,
    that might reduce trade. Especially if there's a
    snowstorm. And if you can only read tarot during
    the full moon, that's only one day/night a month.
    That's not very good for trade. And what if that's a
    Tuesday? People like to stay home and rent movies
    on Tuesdays, so going out for a tarot reading isn't
    really in the cards. I think this rule is romantic and
    somewhat magical, but not very practical. Espe-
    cially if you want to make a living reading tarot
    cards. One day a month, you have to have a lot of
    really good-paying readings on that day, or you'll
    probably starve.

◊   *When doing a reading with tarot cards, the deck must
    be cut three times, from right to left with the left hand
    before laying out the cards. This distinguishes a tarot
    reading from mere gaming or fortune telling.* We all
    know gaming with a tarot deck is wrong, so we
    understand this rule in that context. Fortune tell-
    ing is what charlatans do, and isn't the same as a
    'real' tarot reading. Charlatans will tell you any-
    thing they think you want to hear, as long as you
    pay their fee. Tarot readers only tell the truth as
    shown by the cards. Tarot readers are superior to

others who just trifle with the tarot, and don't you forget it!

DIGRESSION #2

In the REAL history of Tarot and divination with playing cards, there is a period when various playing cards were used for fortune telling, starting in France with Etteilla before 1770. He first started with a piquet deck—a regular deck of playing cards minus the pips of 2-6—a deck with 32 cards. He assigned meanings to each card, and added another card—the Etteilla—to represent the querant—the person getting the reading.

Shortly thereafter Etteilla got a Tarot deck—the deck used for the game—and after rearranging and redesigning several cards, and numbering each card in the deck from 1 to 77 (reserving the Fool for the querant), he created a deck designed solely for telling fortunes. Others soon copied/ ripped off his idea and began telling fortunes as well. This practice of fortune telling became a fad widely practiced in Paris and other French towns and was widely regarded as something either to be enjoyed, or reviled. Mostly it was considered that the people who went to fortune tellers were women, gullible and somewhat less than serious or scholarly. Certainly they weren't scholars of esoteric wisdom. At least that's what the scholars of serious esoteric wisdom told themselves. The wider culture embraced fortune-telling and several persons became quite wealthy and famous telling fortunes to the rich and famous, as well as anyone who had the coin to get their fortune told. There were scandals about nobles believing fortune tellers and rumors abounded about who told what to whom and what came of it. It was a big deal, and as hot a popular fad as mood rings, pet rocks or the Kardassians.

Eventually the French Revolution came about, and fortune telling was still popular, and then Napoleon came around, and he and his also found the fad useful. Then Napoleon was defeated at Waterloo, and the fad died slowly, as popular fads will. However the bad air surrounding 'fortune telling' stayed. And in some way it persists to this day. Fortune telling is considered to be frivolous, somewhat suspect and possibly outrightly criminal. Certainly the esotericists consider 'mere fortune telling' to be a bad thing.

Napoleon discards a reading

When Court de Gébelin spied that Tarot card (The World, for those who have been paying attention) he was certainly aware of the fortune telling fad. He was an esotericist, and not at all interested in fads. He was a serious scholar of the Western Magical Tradition. So when he took that deck and started assigning meanings to various cards, he made sure he distanced himself from 'mere' fortune-telling. And he used the tarot deck as he found it—no reassigning cards or renumbering or anything suspect like that. He used only the trumps—the Major Arcana—in part to distance himself from those charlatan fortune tellers who used a different card deck—though theirs wasn't a regular tarot deck.

And that snooty air still persists around Tarot readings to this day. A tarot reader is someone who is a student of the Western Magical Tradition in some way, and they would never stoop to 'mere' fortune telling—it's a sacred thing and never to be profaned by saying what the person wants to hear. That's what fortune tellers do. Not real tarot readers.

End Digression #2. Back to the lore.

◊ *When doing a tarot reading, after properly shuffling and cutting the cards, the client should blow lightly on the deck, and slap it once, lightly, before the cards are laid out in the spread.* This is to get the client's energy into the deck. Except they already have shuffled (13 times) and cut the deck (into 3 piles from right to left with their left hand), so I think their energy is thoroughly in the deck already. Blowing on and slapping the deck? What kind of cockamamie stuff are we into here? That's just weird. Nothing weird about tarot cards. Magic, but never weird.

◊ *You should only learn tarot from a qualified teacher, and do what they tell you. Experimentation could be dangerous!* This one totally ignores the 'tarot readers are born not made' crowd—so we will too. Like my logic? You ignore me, I'll ignore you! If only life could be as peaceful as that.

Easy to tell where this rule came from: the people who teach tarot. Now aside from the question of exactly who is a qualified tarot teacher (I know I am for sure!) what about all those people who learned tarot from books, as I did because there were no tarot teachers around—qualified or not—when I was learning? Now they're seemingly everywhere. Is a book considered a qualified tarot teacher? Certainly we know everything in books is true. And most tarot decks come with a book—usually in a boxed set with book and deck and sometimes a nice little bag to put the cards in as well. So learning from a book vs. learning from a teacher? Which is better? Depends on whether you write or sell books, or teach tarot in classes. If you do both, well there's something said about having your cake and eating it too.

Certainly the 'experimentation is dangerous' statement is true. It's just self-evident. Tarot cards are magic and you shouldn't fool around with magical stuff. You need to be reverent and respectful because if you trifle with dangerous energies, and you do something wrong, the cards could explode. Remember all the earlier warnings? They still apply.

11 Fixing a 'Broken' Deck

So what do you do if you manage to make a mistake—and survive it—and you end up with a deck with all the magic gone? Can you save your deck, or are you doomed to have a dead deck for the rest of your life?

Luckily, there are a couple of rules addressing all this.

If your deck loses all or even some of its magic, you can place your deck in the light of a full moon to recharge the cards. Whew—there is a way to save your deck. Bet you were worried about this. I know I was, once.

Deck being recharged in the moonlight

Now this rule is nice, but it doesn't go far enough. Do you place the deck in the bag, or wrapped in silk, or in its box in the full moonlight? And if the deck should be bare and unwrapped—as I would interpret this rule most strictly—what if the wind blows and your cards get scattered everywhere? If they touch the ground or floor or bare table the magic can leak out, thereby negating this restorative trick. Full moonlight is a nice thing, and magical (and you know that!) but they don't get specific enough about how to do this. And if you can only do readings during the full moon, when will you be able to recharge your deck? Very frustrating.

If someone other than a designated person touches your cards and steals the magic out of them, you can bury them overnight in the earth to cleanse them. Again this is a relief, because I worry about all those potentially polluted decks hanging around out there.

But again, the rule isn't specific enough. Are the cards buried wrapped in silk, or in the bag, or in the box? If the silk/bag/box is designed to protect the magic in the cards, how can the magic migrate back into the cards if they are in something designed to protect the cards from stray energies? And if the cards touch the ground, the magic can leak out of them. Or is it just the surface of the ground? Maybe the surface of the ground will pull the magic out, and putting the cards beneath the surface of the ground will allow cards buried there to reclaim all the magic that leached out when any cards touched the ground. But burying unprotected cards can get messy—especially if it rains and they end up buried in the mud. One author states you should wrap your deck in cotton cloth before burying them in the ground. This solves the muddy deck problem.

This one may derive from Orthodox Judaism. They have utensils specially designated for meat and milk, and if the wrong person touches them, or they are used for the wrong thing, they can be buried for a time, and they will be cleansed. Everyone knows tarot cards have correspondences to Kabbalah, and the Kabbalah is Jewish, so it all stands to reason. Keep polishing that sterling research, there!

DIGRESSION #3

So all this hoopla about the deck itself and nothing about the cardboard box it comes in.

Why not? The box is made from similar materials to the deck and usually has a picture of one or more of the cards on it. That makes it as magic as the cards themselves, right?

Beat-up tarot box

The pictures themselves are magic, we all know that. So what do you do with the box? Do you put the cards in the original cardboard box, then the silk cloth, then the bag, then the special wooden box? What happens when the cardboard box disintegrates from use, as all cardboard boxes do with a well-used deck? Do you save the pieces? Certainly to just throw it away would be a bad thing, and the Tarot Police™ would use it as a black mark against you. Wonder how many black marks lead to an actual visit? I certainly don't want to find out directly.

See how these do's and don'ts lead to many problems? That's why I wrote this book, to help clear up all these questions. I certainly hope you appreciate all my hard work here. Hey, you bought the book, I guess that's enough.

End of Digression #3.

If your deck is giving you confused impressions, you might need to cleanse it with a smudge and/or crystals. This smudge can be of sage, sandalwood or whatever other 'flavor' you feel will do the trick. Asafetoeta will really do it—but it totally stinks up your house. The smudging techniques vary—some say smudge the deck as you hold it—use a circular motion all around in every direction. Some say the deck should be placed on a table, and the incense be waved in a circular fashion over the deck. Some would have you spread the deck out, and smudge over it ensuring each card is exposed to the smudge. Some say after you have smudged the cards, rest a quartz crystal on top of the deck (in the silk, in the bag, in the box...) to help keep it clean.

Then there's the crystal trick. Instead of smudging, you place a crystal next to the deck, then wrap it in the silk, in the bag, in the box etc. Some say you should use clear quartz, some say smoky quartz. Some say just quartz, and leave the color/variety up to you. Black tourmaline is great for sucking the yuck out of things—tarot cards included. Selenite can be used to 'tune' the deck. There are many different rocks/crystals you could use, but this isn't a rock book, so I'll leave all the rest of the combinations and permutations up to you. If what you choose doesn't work, I think you'll know pretty quickly. Unless you're not psychic enough to tell, and then you shouldn't be using tarot cards anyhow if that's the case. So there!

A *pendulum can be used to cleanse a deck by drawing out negative energies.* No word on what the pendulum should be made of, or how to use it. I guess you just wave it around over the deck until you feel the deck is cleansed enough. And if you can't tell when that is, you probably aren't psychic enough to read tarot anyhow. See how all these important rules fit together? Me neither.

You can immerse your deck in salt to remove any unwanted energies it may have picked up. Or alternatively, set the deck inside an unbroken ring of salt as it rests on a table. This comes from the days when salt was a rare commodity, and extremely valuable. In some societies in history, salt was worth more per ounce than gold. And salt is vital for people to live. You can certainly live without gold, though people who have 'gold fever' will totally dispute that. Salt has always been considered a cleansing and purifying agent. Nowadays salt is cheap and plentiful, so having a big bowl full of salt to immerse your deck in isn't a financial hardship. You could sprinkle salt water over your deck, but that might damage the deck. But the cards are encased in plastic, so maybe a few drops of salt water won't be a big deal. Immersion in salt water is a bad thing. That plastic coating won't stand up to immersion in salt water or plain water—or most any other liquid. Water damaged cards are a pain—they don't shuffle well, they are warped and sometimes crumpled, and are just sad. I feel sorry for decks that have been water damaged.

Clearing the deck before and after a reading session is done by placing the deck face down on a table, holding your hands over the deck, palms down and crossed at the wrists, and then

quickly separating your hands with a forceful gesture. This supposedly casts out negative or unwanted vibes. It's not a full
cleansing, but more of a psychic 'wipe down' to get surface
energies off the deck. It supposedly prepares your cards
for the next reading. At least this one has the advantage
of being quick and easy.

A broken deck will haunt you

12 Do's and Don'ts of Readings

Up to now we have only explored the lore of tarot as it pertains to the history and the deck of cards itself. Now we talk about the lore surrounding actually doing readings. Get cozy—there is a lot of it. (Yeah, there sure is a lot of it in this book!)

You can only ask a question once, and once you get your answer, that's it. If you ask again you are profaning the tarot and things could get grim. Or alternatively the magic will leak out of the cards.

Estelle knows

Ooh, ooh! <<Estelle raises her hand and jumps up and down>>

Being an astrologer, I know the answer to this one. In astrology there's a branch called horary (not hoary or horrid, though both adjectives have been used about it), (That joke never gets old...) which is the astrology of divination. You ask a question, and a chart is cast for the date, time and place the astrologer receives and under-stands the question. One of the rules of horary astrology is that you can only ask a question once, and get the answer and that's it. No do-overs. If it's good enough for horary astrology, it should be good enough for tarot. Astrology is magic and horary astrology is especially magic so it really applies

72

to tarot also because tarot and astrology have correspondences. Eliphas Levi and Aleister Crowley said so, and we
all know they always told the truth about everything.

You can ask only one question per session. No multiple questions, no re-shuffling, no follow-ups. Once is enough.

Obviously some tarot reader who wanted to limit how
long they would stay with one client made this one up. It's
an old rule, probably obsolete, because nowadays most tarot
readers charge by the minute, not the reading. They want
you to stay as long as possible, so doing multiple readings
means more money for them.

*When doing a reading, the client must ask the question ver-
bally—otherwise the tarot reader is just questing in the dark and
cannot hone in on the proper meaning of the reading.*

*When doing a reading the client shouldn't have to ask the
question—the tarot reader should be psychic enough and the
cards magical enough to clearly show the question and answer
without 'hints'.*

Two more mutually exclusive rules. Some of this comes
from style—there are readers who like to amaze the client
by just using the cards and totally telling the client what
their question was, and giving an uncannily accurate valuable answer. Then there are readers who like to have a
clue beforehand, and use that to refine and hone the card
meanings for that specific question. And then there are
the times when the cards are answering another question
entirely—one that the client didn't consciously think about,
but is on their subconscious mind and they are happy to get
that answer, even though they didn't know they needed it.
Aren't the cards just magic? They can do the most amazing
things!

If while shuffling a card falls out or is accidentally turned over, the reading is spoiled and you have to start over, or maybe come back on another day. Obviously you want the reading to be good, correct and done properly. Cards that fall out are just screwing up the magic and profaning the reading. Better get them into that moonlight or the Tarot Police™ will come to get you!

You must read all reversals. Read the Cards as they lie.

You must read all cards upright, if one gets turned around the reading may be spoiled, but you can also turn it upright and maybe if you do it quickly and smudge, it will be okay.

So these last two are mutually exclusive again. Lots of that in tarot lore. Now are you understanding why I really needed to write this book (apart from needing the money)? Well, one or the other, take your pick. They can't both be right, or can they?

If during a reading, you turn a card around so it is upside-down to the client, you are hexing them. Tarot cards are magic and hexing is bad magic, so I guess you can do bad magic things with tarot cards. But we know that. This book is all about the good and bad things you should and shouldn't do with the cards. Now, will this hexing also cause the magic in the deck to go bad, or leak out or explode? We want the cards to be happy and good, and not have the magic be bad, or profaned or anything unfortunate, so better not do this one. We want everything to be good and happy and done properly. No hexing allowed!

Respectable tarot readers don't hex

13 LORE SURROUNDING SPREADS

Once you get your deck you also usually get a book, either the little one packed with the deck inside the cardboard box (the little white book—AKA LWB), or the full-sized book in the deck-book set box. And in that book, there are spreads—illustrated ways to lay out the cards, and what each position means, and possibly when to use each spread.

The reading is the reading, you cannot do more or differently than the spread as published. All spreads are set in stone. Everyone knows spreads are sacred and special. People much smarter, more psychic and just plain better than you are created those spreads (no Gypsies from Egypt here) and you'd just better do them as they were originally intended, or bad things could happen to you.

The Tarot Police™ only use land line

I personally know this is an area where the Tarot Police™ take great interest. They want to make sure the cards are used properly, and screwing up spreads can cause bad things to happen. How do I know? Well, while writing this book, I got a phone call, and the muffled voice on the other end told me (couldn't tell if it was male or female) they were aware of my work, and they would answer a few questions in the spirit of getting the message out so they won't have to intervene as often. And they let me know, in no uncertain terms, that screwing around with spreads as published in books is absolutely forbidden. If it's in a book it's true and important—so everyone better just pay attention here. Got that? I sure did.

The Celtic Cross is the best/only spread for reading tarot. 'Nuff said. It's the most widely published spread, and it always works. Really. I said so, and it's in a book so it's true, right?

You can only do the big readings/the full deck readings once a year. This one is because many readers are sick of those whole-deck readings and so want to limit their use. Also they can't usually charge much more for them, and they want to maximize their number of clients, and if they spend all their time with one person doing a big reading, they can't do a lot of people in a short time. Whatever. It's a rule, so pay attention!

You cannot read for yourself, you can only read for others. This is because you never can be as objective about yourself as you can be with other people. Except most people learn to read tarot by reading for themselves before they jump to reading for others—usually friends and family first, and then the general public later. I just report this stuff, I don't make it up. (Well, not that much...)

If you do read for yourself, you have to have a special deck just for reading for yourself, and another deck you use to read for others. Even if you have another copy of the same deck, you still need two decks and have to keep them separate and distinct.

So this one violates the *'you can have only one deck and you are married to it for life'* rule. Probably has to do with energies and getting them mixed and/or screwed up. But it does allow for more tarot decks being sold. Take it or leave it.

If you have to use the book to get the meanings, it can't be a good reading. You have to be naturally psychic and intuitively understand the cards, so the book should be useless or redundant and completely unnecessary. This goes with the *'if you aren't psychic enough you shouldn't be using tarot cards in the first place'* school of thought. Yeah, and if you took lessons from a qualified tarot teacher you shouldn't need the book anyhow. And don't worry, if you are magical enough you will attract a magical teacher to you.

Doing a reading with a book is soooo wrong....

You must only read and use the book that goes with your specific deck. Other books cannot be right or valid, especially if they depict decks other than your own. This is just self-evident. Just as all tarot decks are magical and special, so each individual book is magical and has its own special energies. Using another book is just wrong and bad and you could cause the magic to leak out of your deck by using the wrong book. And if the book shows several decks simultaneously... I think the Tarot Police™ have this one in hand. After all, there really aren't any books that show more than one deck out there.

Except there are. A lot of very good books. Funny how the Tarot Police™ have missed those. Most decks nowadays come in a big boxed set with a special book depicting that deck. Sometimes they explain the symbolism, usually they have a number of spreads with definitions and explanations, they always have meanings for the cards, upright and reversed and possibly a general paragraph about the idea behind each card, the suits, the Major and Minor Arcana, and all the rest. You can usually get the decks without the special book and bigger box, but retailers discourage that because they can charge more for the set than they can for just the deck. I think you can figure out what's powering this rule.

Eden Gray, Arthur Waite, Papus, Court de Gébelin, Eliphas Levi, Aleister Crowley etc. etc. is the ONLY true tarot authority and everyone else is crap. This is a bunch of individual rules lumped into one. Obviously there can be only ONE Tarot Authority™ and everyone else is crap. But which one? Yeah, I don't know either. Everyone has their favorites, and the people that they think are crap. Like which decks are icky, there is no consensus on this.

Generic tarot books are crap—only deck-specific books are valid. Again, this is put forward by the people who write deck-specific books and make money selling same. On the other hand, there are a lot of tarot books that aren't deck-specific, and they have a lot of really good and valid information. Like this book, which is not deck-specific, and is chock-full of great and valuable information, interesting stories, and digressions.

Yep, I'm sure. This rule is pure crap. Feel free to ignore it. I have it on great authority—just like Papus and all the others. Keep polishing that sterling research!

Big tarot book

Small cheater books—AKA the Little White Book or LWB—are crap, only real full-sized books are valid. Now some people really do swear by this one. The small cheater book, or little white book, that comes in the small box containing the deck itself is usually brief, sometimes in multiple languages, and has really tiny print. Books in multiple languages are suspect anyhow because we all know the universal language of tarot is English. Well, everything I've read about tarot has been in English. It stands to reason. And having tiny print and being abbreviated they can't have lots of good information. Any real book has a cover and proper pages and all that. And once you've opened the box and removed the deck and LWB, it's really hard to get the deck and tiny book back in the box neatly. It's a tight fit for sure. Easier to throw the little white book out, and use the extra room for the cards so they stay nice longer. And if you bought a boxed set, you usually have a special bigger book, so that little book is redundant. But sometimes decks in boxed sets don't have the small cheater book, and that's another proof that small cheater books are bad and wrong.

Little cheater book

14 Rules for Proper Reading Ambiance

Before doing a reading, the reader must wash thoroughly, preferably in running water, and abstain from meat and alcohol for three days beforehand. Whew! That's a lot of preparation and planning for a reading. If you are a professional reader, I guess you have to be a teetotaler vegetarian, because you could do a reading most anytime, and can't wait for three days every time a client calls. I guess tarot cards are vegan after all.

I have nothing against readers being clean, we want people to think well of us, and being dirty and smelly tends

Unclean tarot reader

to make people not want to be around you. And we certainly aren't geeks who don't wash properly. So washing thoroughly is good. Preferably in running water—does that mean tarot readers are confined to showers? No baths allowed? Now this no alcohol or meat for three days beforehand, well a reader's diet may affect their breath, but I think this one may be a bit excessive. One wonders if there were lots of dirty, drunk, meat-eating tarot readers

running around in the past, and this rule was devised to clean them all up, so to speak. Maybe this is another fortune tellers (bad) vs. proper tarot readers (good) rule. We want to be on the side of the good guys, so we want to be clean.

When you do a reading, you must light a candle. This is because tarot is magic and lighting a candle looks more magical, so they just have to go together. Just be careful you don't set anything, like your cards, or book, or silk scarf, on fire. Or drip wax on anything—like the cards, or your book, or your silk cloth, or the bag, or your special wooden box, or yourself. This is the Gypsy Reader theory. If it looks magical, it makes the reading better. Trappings are good and make the mark—er, client—believe in your magic powers more.

Some people have special clothing they wear when doing readings. The people who wear the special shawls, headdresses, robes, jewelry, or whatever are inherently more magical because they look more magical than a person in regular street clothes. If it looks more magical, it IS more magical. And is a better reading. Everyone knows if you look psychic you ARE psychic. P. T. Barnum knew all about this one for sure.

You must cast a circle before you do a reading. This is to keep the magic in the cards, and makes a special place for doing readings. Tarot is magic and circles are magic, so they should go together. If you don't protect the magic the reading won't be valid.

Now this one can be practical and useful. A magical circle, properly cast will keep out any extraneous influences and energies and psychic noise, and may allow you to get a better more clear reading. Try it, you might be surprised. Alternatively, if you don't want to go to all the bother, you can still do a reasonably good reading if you concentrate on it.

You must light incense when you do a reading. This is to help set the ambiance, make a nice smell and generally help make the reading special. Some people advocate waving the incense over the cards before you shuffle them, to cleanse them in preparation for the reading, I guess. If you are casting a circle, then you may already have the incense.

Dressed for tarot success

Some people also say you need to lay out an assortment of crystals to define the limits of your circle. This is getting awfully elaborate. And if you do readings outside your home, you suddenly have a whole box of stuff you need to cart around for your readings, in addition to the cards themselves. This sort of defeats the idea that card reading is relatively simple because all you need is the deck and a flat surface.

You must never read for parties, just for fun, or for entertainment purposes. This profanes the sacred and ancient knowledge contained in the cards. Tarot is magic, and magic is serious, so you have to be serious about doing tarot readings.

Lots of tarot readers make good money doing parties and such. They usually get a flat fee, and do a reading for whoever wants one, for a specific length of time. It's a living, and many people who put on parties like to have such entertainments available for their guests. So whether or not you subscribe to this rule depends on how you like to make money. Most professional readers will take most any gig that pays well.

If you read in public, you must prominently display a disclaimer that the reading is for entertainment purposes only. Many municipalities have laws against fortune telling. These laws are designed to protect the public from a certain type of confidence scheme which centers around fortune telling of various types, and can result in the victim being cheated out of thousands of dollars in various ways. It's fraud, pure and simple. Unfortunately, the line between what looks like fraudulent activity/fortune telling and a proper tarot reading is hazy. So many readers have signs which they display prominently that their services are 'for entertainment purposes only'. This allows them to do readings and not get arrested for fraudulent activities. All in good fun, doncha know. Whatever keeps you out of jail. This one is based in pure practicality, so do what you will.

If it keeps you out of jail...

A *true tarot reader must never charge for readings.* This is another filthy lucre rule. Some people believe that to charge for something profanes it. Tarot is magic and magic is spiritual and spiritual stuff cannot be pure if you pay for it. Um, what about giving at a church? Or tithing? Doesn't that have to do with spiritual stuff? Yeah, whatever. The people who make money doing readings for money (be it by the reading or more lucratively, by the minute) obviously don't pay attention to this rule.

If a client wants to make a free-will offering, well, that's some-thing else entirely. You can only graciously accept whatever they give you. Yeah, sure. Use semantics to obfuscate and make it okay to take money without profaning yourself by 'charging' for a reading. Look, if you want to charge, then charge directly for your readings, but don't be coy about it by having free will offerings. Besides, you will probably get more if you state your fee upfront. And if they want to tip you extra, well you can accept that, too.

You must pay for a tarot reading to show respect for the reader. Now money isn't filthy lucre—it's respect. So to charge or not to charge? Depends if you need the money, I guess. Certainly all tarot readers deserve respect—as do people who write books about tarot. Respect is a good thing. You paid for this book, so I accept your respect, and I thank you. Respect is good. So is money. Remember, if you're burdened by too much money, just send it along to me and I'll take care of it for you. I'm happy to provide this public service, really.

Tarot cards must never be mixed with any other divinatory system. Like other tarot decks, or other divinatory type decks, or other divinatory systems whatsoever. If you do, both become invalid and the magic leaks out of two things, and that's a lot of magic leaking all over and what could happen is just too awful to contemplate—you could have an explosion—or the Tarot Police™ will come to get you— or you could become possessed. Whew! That's a lot of bad things that could happen. Better just leave it all alone and read tarot by itself.

Except many people—even the original authors of received tarot lore—all state that tarot had a strong correlation with Kabbalah, astrology, numerology, alchemy and other magical, mystical and esoteric systems. Tarot cards contain all the magical and mystical knowledge of the Egyptians, Gypsies, Ancient Greece, Rome, Hebrews, Moses, the Templars, Persians, Arabic cultures, Atlantis and anything else I can't think of at the moment but which could plausibly be lumped into the categories of magical, mystical, occult and secret, but neat.

Hmmm. However can we reconcile this correlation with

the *'don't mix tarot with anything else'* rule? We can either take it as valid, and never mix our one-and-only tarot deck with any other deck or system, or ignore it and risk the consequences. After all tarot cards were invented by Ancient Egyptian Priests and they knew way better than you what was an appropriate ingredient for the cards, so they can contain all the great esoteric knowledge of the world. Or Europe. Or the Gypsies. Or Life, the Universe and Everything. Whatever.

DIGRESSION #4

So what makes a deck true tarot, and what about other divinatory decks? There are sure a lot of decks out there—some calling themselves tarot, and some not.

As I stated before, a true tarot deck has 78 cards: 56 cards AKA the Minor Arcana, made up of 4 suits of 14 cards each—10 pips numbered ace – 10 (and they may or may not have special pictures for each pip) plus 4 court cards per suit, Page, Knight, Queen and King; and another suit of trumps—AKA the Major Arcana of 22 cards numbered and named. Supposedly if a deck deviates from this time-honored pattern, it is not a true tarot deck. And therefore not magical or containing all the knowledge of Western Occultism.

There are many different decks of divinatory systems. There are domino cards, mahjong cards, I Ching cards, Kabbalah cards, astrology cards and various other systems of divination converted into cards.

Then there are also shaman cards, power animal cards,

angel cards, psychology cards, dream cards, Zener cards (used to test psychic ability) and whatever else a person might think up to turn into a divinatory deck. There are sure a whole lot of them out there.

Lots of choices

Some of these variant decks use the word 'tarot' in their title, but are not tarot. The Tarot Police™ told me that they have enough to do without having to enforce what non-tarot decks may or may not be OK. I trust that shadowy voice, so I'll take this one as received truth. I received it by listening on the phone. So there. Keep polishing that sterling research. Eventually it will shine all pretty.

A person who wants to buy a tarot deck might have a bit of trouble determining if a deck is really a true tarot deck or not. This is where the various tarot sites around the web are really useful. Many describe and rate decks, so if you look it up on the internet first, you can discover if that deck you love and want to buy is really tarot, or some aberration just using (and possibly abusing) tarot's good name. Of course, if you actually bought it and discovered afterward it wasn't a real tarot deck, it doesn't count against only owning one deck at a time or whatever you choose to believe.

So a savvy person will know that not everything that calls itself tarot, or is a card deck, is really tarot. Caveat emptor. You remember what that means, don't you? Okay, it means 'let the buyer beware' in Latin. The quickest way to tell if a deck is true tarot is to look on the back, and see how many cards are in the deck. If it's 78, you have a good chance you've got a real tarot deck. If there's a different number, it probably isn't.

End of Digression #4.

Beware, buyer!

15 LORE ABOUT POSSESSION FROM TAROT

If you burn a tarot deck, you can hear the voices scream as it burns. These voices are supposedly the voices of the damned souls trapped in the cards, and when burned are released from the deck to go into hell. Go to Hell—go directly to Hell—do not pass go—do not stay in purgatory—just go to Hell.

Screaming souls leaving the deck

This one comes from the fundamentalists, popularized and spread far and wide by Pat Robertson on his show the 700 Club. According to him, everyone knows tarot (pronounced by him as **tear**-ott) cards are occult (pro-nounced by him as **aww**-kult) and therefore satanic—at least according to Pat Robertson and those who believe as he does. Sigh. Yeah, various belief systems do not agree on many things, and tarot cards are one of the more prominent ones. After all, the cards show the Devil, so they have to be satanic. Except there are several angels, the resurrection, and many other prominently Christian symbols contained therein—so I guess the Devil is so awfully satanic he can wipe out all the angelic energies contained in tarot also. Whatever floats your boat. Or sinks it in this instance.

I would guess that if you are a fundamentalist Evangelical Christian you probably won't read this book, it being about those evil satanic tarot cards and all.

I can personally comment on this bit of lore.

Yet Another Tarot Story

I was attending a Midsummer ritual in the early '90's and part of the ritual was a great bonfire. Okay, it was in a big cauldron out-side, but it was a pretty big fire anyway. We had created boons drawn on paper, and part of the ritual was to cast those boons into the fire so they could be sent up to heaven and hopefully be read and acted upon by the Gods. This is a classic burnt offering.

One participant had a deck of tarot cards he wanted to dispose of. They had been a gift from a person he was on the outs with, he didn't want them in his house or his life anymore, and he wanted to sever the ties between him-self and the person who gave them to him. So he cast the cards, a few at a time, into the Midsummer fire. Watching tarot cards being cast into a fire and burnt was traumatic for me. I collected cards from my teens, had several dozen decks at that time, and was greatly upset at the thought of burning a deck. I understood what he was doing and why, but watching those cards being cast into the fire and burnt was still a difficult thing for me.

Throwing cards into the fire

That being said, neither I, nor anyone else around that fire, heard any screaming or moaning or anything other than normal fire sounds as the cards burnt to ash. So this whole 'souls screaming as they are released and sent directly to hell' seems to be hogwash. We didn't see anything either, and maybe we should have as the magic in the cards would have been released as they were burnt... I did say it was traumatic, so maybe I was too traumatized to see the magic being released. Yeah, that's it. I was too traumatized. That's my story and I'll stick to it.

End of story. Back to more lore about possession.

If you use tarot cards too much, or in a wrong manner, you could become possessed yourself. This can be another corollary from Pat Robertson and Co., but could also be true.

My mom is an interesting person, and always encouraged me with the astrology and tarot stuff. Once when visiting her, she had a friend over who also read tarot, and this friend related to me a story of becoming possessed because (so she said) she had used her cards 'too much'. I was surprised, and as she related the story, it became readily apparent that not only wasn't she getting enough sleep, or food, or taking care of herself in other ways, she was also doing other psychic practices which could result in possession. So whether it was the tarot cards, or the lack of self-care and the other risky psychic practices, couldn't be determined definitively. Yes, the cards were involved, but in over 40+ years of working with tarot and talking with other tarot practitioners and enthusiasts and collectors, its' the ONLY story I've heard about possession first hand. Hearsay accounts from Pat Robertson aren't really admissible in court. Make up your own mind yourself.

When you read tarot the genius of the deck sits on your shoulder and tells you which cards to choose. Genius? What the heck? Okay here's the deal—genius is a word which has older more classical meanings than the way we use it now—a person of extraordinary intelligence. Originally it meant a spirit, elemental or other para-normal 'intelligence' associated with a person, place or thing. It's the same cognate as genie or jinn. (For once the 'sounds like' rule does actually work for word meanings!) It is a sort of thought-form that helps your mind and psyche with para-normal stuff. Like tarot cards.

So every deck supposedly has a genius, and when you open it up this small entity sits on your shoulder and whispers in your ear. Things are getting crowded in that little box. The deck, the cheater book, the magic, and now a small para-normal entity that magically jumps up and sits on your shoulder once you open the deck. And obviously that genius follows the deck, even after the box has disintegrated and you have only the bare deck—wrapped in silk, of course. In a bag, in a box, etc. etc. etc.

The Genius of the deck

Again, here is something the fundamentalists can latch onto and declare tarot decks satanic. The dictionary definition of genius says nothing about satan—the original meanings date from a time before satan was invented by the Jews and Christians—classical Greece to be precise. But a little 'guy' sitting on your shoulder telling you which cards to pull sounds a bit creepy. I have never experienced this one, but I guess some people feel they do hear voices when they read tarot, and who am I to disabuse them of their impressions?

Every time you open a new tarot deck, a demon leaps out to claim your soul for using tarot cards. This seems to be the flip side of the 'genius' rule. And that box is now still more crowded, with the deck, LWB cheater book, magic, genius and/or demon. The demon jumps out when you first open the deck, but it does not live permanently in the deck. Once released, the demon is gone, supposedly taking your soul with it back to hell, which is where all demons live.

Demon leaping out of the deck

This is another one the fundamentalists seem to like and spread around a lot. And demons are servants of satan, so with this one they can totally latch onto and claim tarot cards are satanic. Sometimes even tarot sellers spread this lore around in mockery of the fundamentalists and their superstitions. Demon or genius, I still have never seen anything jump out of a tarot deck when I open it. So maybe this is just an urban legend, spread by fundamentalists, and mocked by tarot sellers. I tried to check it out on Snopes (www.snopes.com), but there's nothing about tarot there. Believe what you will.

Something else that can jump out at you

16 More Lore About Tarot Itself

The REAL mysteries are in the Minor Arcana—the pip cards. This one goes around tarot circles from time to time. The pictures on the pips do show more everyday and useful stuff than the Major Arcana—the trumps—do, in many people's opinion. Really, how often do we see the devil, or a lady holding a lion's mouth closed, or a chariot pulled by two sphinxes? Think about it.

I guess this one is a matter of what you consider magical and useful. Unfortunately, the first fully pictorial tarot pips came from illustrated game decks in Germany, not decks used for divination. During the Victorian era, tarot jumped the channel and ended up in England where a Great Western Occult Revival was happening. The knowledge of the game of tarot was unknown in England—it was never really played there much—so seeing these fully pictorial decks—originally created for the game—and translating this into the occult and divinatory use of tarot—which had started less than 100 years previously in France, and then moved to England (which was the center of the world at the time)—translated into a few rare fully pictorial tarot decks for divination. Up to then most all tarot decks—and certainly all the tarot decks used for divination—had pips with only the suit marker in the appropriate number, e.g. the 9 of coins depicted 9 coins and little else.

There was an old deck—the Sola Busca deck from Northern Italy in the late 1400's—that did have scenes on the pips. It was in the British Museum, and available for viewing. But from that deck through the 1700's pips had been plain—they depicted only the number of whatever suit symbol they were.

Non-pictorial cards, having only pips

In the early 1900's Arthur Edward Waite—an occultist and former member of the Golden Dawn, the organization through which all Western Occultism was channeled, disseminated, codified and re-worked in many ways—decided to commission a tarot deck that contained all the 'correct' symbols of the original trumps. He was very specific about what those cards would look like and exactly which symbols they would contain. He felt the 'original' tarot trumps had been somewhat altered and watered down through the centuries, and he wanted to return the trumps to their original occult power and significance. This was still in the days when everybody believed in *'the magical tarot from the Gypsies by way of Egypt'* received lore. They didn't know any better.

He retained Pamela Colman Smith to draw this deck— another member of the Golden Dawn and a commercial artist. She drew the trumps to Waite's specifications. But for the rest of the cards, Waite gave her free reign to draw what she chose. She may have gone to the British Museum and viewed that old Sola Busca deck for inspiration, but we don't know. In Pamela's deck, each suit depicts a story in the images of the pips. She drew a fully pictorial tarot deck deliberately designed for divination and nothing else. In 1909—a momentous year—this deck was published by the printing company of Rider and Co.—and so the Rider Waite tarot deck was born. It is the definitive tarot deck of the 20th century. It has supposedly never been out of print from 1909 to the present, under various publishers in Britain, Europe and since 1971 by U.S. Games in the U.S.

Rider Waite is the 'template' deck from which many others are based, either deliberately or unconsciously. When describing decks, reviewers usually state if the deck is Rider Waite derived or not. To people who use and collect tarot, it matters. So people of the 20th century had as their main template a fully pictorial deck, which was widely printed, sold and marketed. When people talk about tarot, these images are the ones used to illustrate the various cards. They are very familiar to most people who are even only marginally aware of tarot. Whether or not the pips have more special occult magic than the trumps is probably a matter of personal belief. Your choice. I think both groups are equally useful.

Tarot decks with non-pictorial pips are devoid of meaning— only real tarot has fully pictorial pips. If you paid attention to the preceding paragraphs, you know the original tarot decks had non-pictorial pips, and fully pictorial pips were 'standardized' by the Rider Waite deck. This one comes from people who make and sell fully pictorial tarot decks. Or people who grew up with Rider Waite and don't know about other older non-pictorial decks. Or maybe they do know, but prefer the fully pictorial pips. Realistically, fully pictorial pips are easier to read—each having a distinct picture makes it easier to attach a meaning to the card rather than 3 vs. 4 swords on cards.

The elemental correspondence for the suits is: wands are fire, cups are water, swords are air and pentacles are earth.

The elemental correspondence for the suits is: wands are air, cups are water, swords are fire and pentacles are earth.

Another mutually exclusive set of rules. Interesting that nobody really disputes cups being water—well duh!—and pentacles being earth. Some decks are designed with the correlation for wands to fire and swords to air, and others have it vice versa. Each manages to make a strong case for their own right and true correlation. I guess if you use a certain deck, then you should follow the correspondence that was 'built' into that deck. People still have fist fights and flame wars about it, though. Makes for lively parties at tarot conventions.

The real original tarot deck has 5 suits—4 suit decks are 'stripped down' from the original. Again, this one circulates in tarot circles from time to time.

There is a deck called the Mantegna deck, designed in Italy in the late 1400's, that had 5 suits of 10 cards each, with no extra trumps. These cards were numbered from 1 to 50 and depicted things like the sun, moon and stars, arts, muses and other things sometimes found in regular tarot decks. But without the extra suit of trumps, this is not a tarot deck, 5 suits notwithstanding. History does not record the game played with this particular deck.

There are a couple of tarot decks with 5 suits—92+ card decks. The 5th suit supposedly corresponds to spirit. But these decks are definitively much later than the original playing cards in the 1100's and the original tarot decks in the 1400's. The ones I know of are all from the 1900's. So this one isn't provable except as esoteric received knowledge. Shiny.

Mamluk Card

There is a deck from India that has 10 suits—one for each of Vishnu's incarnations—used in a game played in Islamic societies. Now apart from the anachronism of Islamics playing a game with a deck depicting the incarnations of a Hindu God, it is a deck which has a long history. But 10 isn't 5, and tarot is not Islamic, and this deck doesn't answer the question about 4 or 5 suits. But it is an interesting factoid. More fun trivia for you!

Any tarot deck with non-standard or extra cards is wrong. A real tarot deck has only 22 Major Arcana, only 56 Minor Arcana, and the court cards are Page, Knight, Queen and King. Supposedly, there is one sacred real and true template for tarot and anything else is wrong, bad and devoid of magic. And the magic is what you are using when reading the cards with tarot, so this rule obviously is right. It just has to be. Somebody said so, I believe it, and that's that. More sterling received wisdom passed on for your enlightenment. It's shiny.

The non-standard card you most often see is substituting a princess or other female figure for the Page—who is usually depicted as a young male. This is so there is a

101

gender balance in the court cards. This one was started by people in the Golden Dawn. When Waite did his deck, Pamela Colman Smith went back to King, Queen, Knight and Page. Other decks change the court cards to something other than King, Queen, Knight and Page. Like father, mother, son and daughter, or other sets of people groups. My non-scientific estimate is that almost 20% of the current decks use alternate figures in some way for court cards. Whether you consider this bad or wrong probably depends upon what deck you are married to. Or whether you design, publish and/or sell decks that have alternate court cards.

The Page and two alternatives

There are decks with extra court cards—5 or 6 court cards per suit. This is to add female cards without eliminating any of the existing male cards. There are many interesting variations here. Probably whatever you can imagine has been done for court cards. And if you can imagine something never done before, maybe you should create your own deck and sell it!

Then there are the decks with different cards for the Major Arcana—the trumps. Decks not based on Rider Waite or other traditional decks can have variant cards for some or even all of the 22 trumps. They are usually theme decks and so use the images, characters and symbology of whatever the special theme of the deck is. If you like and agree with the theme, then these variant trumps work for you. If you don't, then they may seem bad or wrong. If you still buy into the received history of tarot, then only 22 Major Arcana, and only 56 Minor Arcana are allowed, and they must be all the same names and numbers as passed down by the Gypsies/Egyptian Priests etc. Whatever floats your boat, again.

In the Italian Renaissance (for those following the real provable history of tarot) when the trumps were originally 'pasted' onto the 56 card deck, there was no special set of trumps—or even a standardized number of trumps. The Florentine/Minchiate tarot has 40 trumps. Some common card variants are Jupiter and Juno for the High Priest and High Priestess, AKA Pope and Pope Joan/Popess. There are decks with some of the cardinal virtues—Faith, Hope and Charity—of which only Temperance survives. The now-standard tarot trumps seem to have been codified sometime in the 1700's in France. This was before tarot was used for divination.

Examples of common card variants

Then you have the modern decks with extra added trumps. Sometimes this is because the designer wanted to depict other images/archetypes in their deck. Some are because it was a collaborative deck, and they had more than 78 artists—so they allowed the extra artists to draw 'new additional' cards. This is the Fantasy Showcase Tarot rationale. Some add trumps for special magical/numerological/whatever reasons. If you use one of these decks, you obviously don't disagree with these extra cards. Again it's a personal taste thing. Unless you are a purist, and then all this extra stuff is wrong and against the laws of tarot as enforced by the Tarot Police™. Better watch out—they can get you if you're using a proscribed or non-standard deck. It's only a matter of time.

Tarot Police™ at the door

Historical decks which are incomplete and have recreated cards are wrong. This is the Visconti deck and others. Yeah, this is a corollary of the *'if you lose a card you are doing something wrong'* rule. There are several historical decks which are incomplete. People who sell decks are always on the lookout for new decks, and historical decks which are incomplete are easy to use for new decks. But people expect a full 78 card deck, so you hire someone to draw up the missing cards, and you only have to pay them for those few cards—the historical cards are usually out of copyright—so you pay less to produce the deck and make more money proportionally.

Some feel if the deck is incomplete, it is no longer valid. Which is really unfair. These historical tarot decks were painted pictures, usually on paper or cardboard. And paintings do not always survive intact. Especially if they are being used and shuffled while playing games. They wear out. Certainly there are no printed paper decks of cards of any sort surviving from before the 1600's or so. We know thousands of decks were printed before then—from the 1100's onward if you've been paying attention—but because paper is an impermanent medium, so far none of these printed decks has survived the ravages of time. They probably didn't store their decks in wooden boxes, or place them on a shoulder-high shelf near an egress and so they were destroyed. We know they existed because people preached sermons against them, and we also have inventories from printers and others that list these decks. But so far, none have survived. They all wore out from frequent use. Or their magic was profaned and they blew up. Take your pick.

Wands, swords, cups and pentacles are the only correct suits, and others aren't real tarot. These 4 suits are pretty much the same as were copied from the original cards that came over from India in the 1100's. The Indian suits had scimitars instead of straight swords, and spears/polo sticks instead of wands. The swords were straightened in some decks—they are still curved in others. The spears were turned into staves or wands. Cups and coins changed shape and design, but stayed cups and coins/pentacles. As tarot moved from Italy to France, Spain, Switzerland and Germany, sometimes the suits morphed. So you can have bells, acorns, shields, leaves and other different suits. Even Spades, Hearts, Clubs and Diamonds are variants of the original swords, cups, wands and pentacles.

Assorted variant suits used for tarot cards

So over time, there have been many suits for tarot and playing cards. Whether you are married to the four 'traditional' suits for tarot is your choice. The Tarot Police™ had no answers for this controversy. They were worn out with my incessant questions way before we got to this topic. They haven't called back since. Hey, guys, I'm waiting—call me! I have more questions. Really. I need to know the Truth! Call me, please!

Cartoon/anime/comic book non-standard style decks are crap.
There are many decks which are 'gimmick decks' for lack
of a better term. Hello Kitty, Gummi Bears, anime, Tarot
of Baseball and Baseball Tarot (two separate decks) and
many more. These decks were created to sell more decks.
Some are pretty interesting and complete within their
milieu—Tarot of Baseball and Baseball Tarot are interesting
marriages of tarot and baseball. Bats, balls, gloves and bases
are their four suits. But can they ever be magic? Depends
if you're a baseball fan and if you believe baseball can be
magic. Certainly much of the magic went out of baseball
in the steroid era. But then the Red Sox did win the World
Series, so maybe the magic is back. Or maybe you're waiting
for the Cubs to win the Series again. In that case, the magic
may be gone forever. Hey, I lived in Chicago and went to
Cubs games, so I have the right to say this.

Ahem. Baseball notwithstanding, most of these decks
are created as novelties and I know of few people who
read with them. They don't feel magic to me, but then I'm
a collector and supposedly breaking some of the rules as
it is. I'm still keeping a low profile. The Tarot Police™ may
have called me, but they haven't stopped by yet.

Then there are the many decks drawn by comic book
artists—some more well-crafted than others. One publisher
uses a lot of comic book artists, and most of those decks
are pretty good. You should know that I'm also a comic
book collector, so I see nothing wrong with this. I started
collecting comic books way before I ever heard of tarot,
and still have all of my original comics. Nyaaah!!!

Certainly comic book artists are used to producing many
images in a short period of time, so they can create decks
relatively quickly. In the great tradition of Papus, I will rule

107

definitively on this matter: I say these decks are okay and just as magical as the others—remember ALL tarot decks are spritzed with magic at the factory, so all have magic in them from the beginning. I know comic books are okay, I collect them, I also collect tarot decks, and so tarot decks drawn by comic book artists are okay because I said so. There it is. Shiny.

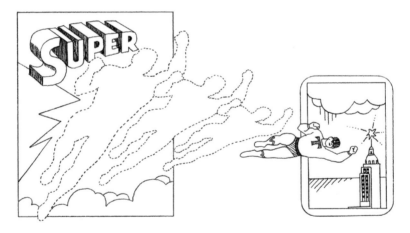

Tarot Man adding respectability to comic book artists

17 SPECIAL LORE ABOUT THE TRUMPS

If no trump cards appear during a reading, then the reading is invalid. One supposes you are using a spread of 5 or more cards here. Statistically, in a 5 card spread, at least one should be a trump. More cards in the spread just increases the possibility for having trumps. But whether you NEED a trump in the spread to make it valid depends on how you view the trumps, I guess. This is a whatever floats your boat kind of rule.

If half the cards in the spread are trumps, then fate is at work and nothing can be done to prevent or change the outcome. Here you have to have a spread with an even number of cards—otherwise you can't get half. Maybe that's a sneaky way of avoiding this rule. So do you believe in fate? What exactly is fate? And how does it operate? "Always in motion is the future"—Yoda. And we all know Jedi Masters are way smarter and more magical than we mortals could ever possibly be. So I guess fate just has to take a back seat to Jedi wisdom.

If all the cards in a spread are trumps, then the client is insane. Again, it all depends on how many cards are in the spread you are using. Realistically, tarot readers are not qualified to make judgment about whether a client is insane or not. And if they are insane, it might not be wise to tell the person that they are. So maybe we can just ignore this rule and move on.

Then we can ask, are you using a full tarot deck to do this reading, or a deck with only the 22 trumps—which was the style of many 18th and 19th century divinatory decks. If you are using only trumps, then duh! Of course the entire reading will be trumps. Rule debunked.

DIGRESSION #5

The first decks used for divination were in the late 1600's in Bologna Italy. The deck used was the Bolognese Tarot—a 62 card deck used for playing games. It has similarities to a regular tarot deck, but some of the trumps are missing, and other cards have different names. A sheet of paper dating before 1750, listing meanings for 35 cards using a Tarot Bolognese deck exists, and is possibly the first written proof of divination using a tarot-derived deck. But it isn't our familiar 78 card tarot deck.

Court de Gébelin was the first we know of to put meanings to the Tarot trumps with regard to divination. His book published in 1781 had essays by himself and Comte de Mellet. Both referenced tarot decks coming from Ancient Egypt, 78 cards, 22 (or 21—sometimes the Fool is apart from the trumps) Trumps and referenced divination using the deck. These essays gave detailed meanings for the trumps, but lots less for the other cards. They also both mentioned the correlation between the 22 trumps and the 22 letters of the Hebrew alphabet.

The next deck used for divination was created before 1770 by Etteilla from a piquet deck—an abbreviated regular 32 card deck, missing the pips 2-6. He moved some cards around and changed the order, and made a few new pictures, and added an extra card—the Etteilla—to depict the client. This was a 33 card deck, published with meanings for the cards. Then Etteilla co-opted de Gebelin and de Mellet's ideas and used them to create his own divinatory deck. It contained 78 cards, and had cards similar to the traditional tarot deck, but he radically changed the order of the trumps and made meanings and pictures for what started as the pips but became somewhat different under Etteilla's designs. This became known as the Grand Etteilla deck. These two Etteilla decks were then copied and imitated, and resulted in several other different divinatory decks that were not tarot. These various decks were printed and widely distributed along with meanings for the cards. Etteilla and his imitators started an industry of cartomancy, known to contemporaries and history as fortune-telling—the first with cards. But it was cartomancy using decks that were not standard tarot—and tarot decks were still mostly used for games—not divination or fortune-telling.

Etteila creating the Grand Etteila

When the world came to discover tarot as a divinatory tool and an adjunct to magical study, using the clues revealed by Court de Gébelin and de Mellet some time in the 1770's or so, it was decided that the most magical cards were the trumps, and so the first magical divinatory decks were trumps-only decks—with 22 cards. At first they used regular playing card tarot decks, discarding the pips and court cards. Later, people designed 22 card trumps-only decks—specifically for divination. This was to differentiate this type of magical divination from that popularized by Etteilla and his imitators, which was considered to be common fortune-telling and not at all suited to esoteric magical work. Divination was serious and intellectual, important, developmental, and used by those who pursued esoteric wisdom. Fortune-telling was common, cheap and used to dupe women, the poor and the gullible. Pure class snobbery, which seems to persist in some circles to this day.

Eliphas Levi with revitalized occultism

When Eliphas Levi went about revitalizing Western European Occultism in the 1850's, he used the tarot cards, and again made correlations between the tarot trumps and the Hebrew alphabet. He gave some meanings for the cards to use in divination. At this time, most divination was done with only the 22 tarot trumps. There were systems using the entire deck, but for the most part, divination was done with 22 card decks only. Etteilla and his imitators had, for the most part, passed out of fashion by this time, but the idea of that kind of cartomancy being common fortune-telling and not desirable for serious magical practitioners still stuck.

And it was mostly that way until Waite redesigned the Tarot deck, and had a deck specially created for divination that had fully pictorial pips. And the Rider Waite deck came with a book by Waite which gave meanings for all 78 cards. So it was easy to use the entire deck for divination, so people started using tarot that way, and nowadays, most people use all 78 cards when doing readings with tarot cards.

End of Digression #5.

Justice must be numbered 8 and Strength must be 11. This is the order we have from antiquity and is the only correct numbering for these cards.

Justice must be numbered 11 and Strength must be 8. This is the order we have from antiquity and is the only correct numbering for these cards.

Ah yes, two more mutually exclusive rules. Here's the real story.

Originally in that standardized deck in France ca. 1700's, Justice was 11 and Strength was 8. Then, some decades later, one deck's maker happened to swap those two trumps—so

Justice became 8 and Strength became 11. No record exists as to why these two trumps were swapped. Maybe someone cut the plates wrong, and they were too cheap to change them. This was another French deck that was very widely distributed, so those 'wrong' trump numbers were copied over and over. They became the 'normal' numbers for a couple centuries. And remember, tarot wasn't used for divination yet, so this numbering had no occult significance at all.

Eliphas Levi had this 'variant' deck when he wrote his books which delineated tarot lore for occult use in the 1850's. So Levi has Justice as 8 and Strength as 11, because that's the way it was in the only deck he knew. And as Modern Western Occultism started with Levi—his correspondences are magical, golden and law. More shiny sterling research here.

Fast forward to the late 1880's and the Golden Dawn. The Golden Dawn was a secret occult society that started in England, though there were also branches in France and Scotland, and that organization managed to collect, codify and update most all of Western Occultism. Part of what they did was to eventually renumber Strength and Justice to better fit for astrological reasons. Remember, tarot is strongly associated with astrology. So starting with Rider Waite and subsequent decks—including Crowley's Thoth Tarot—Strength is 8 and Justice is 11. And because everyone copies Rider Waite, most of the rest of the decks are the same. Except for a few that follow the 'old' order. Nowadays this order is accepted as standard, except all they did was to swap those cards back to the 'original' 'original' way. So which do you use? I'm too confused by this now, choose whichever you want.

The Death card must be unnamed and unnumbered. If you print the name and/or number on it, it means that card can bring real permanent death. Brrr. Creepy to the max! This is the most creepy card in the deck—everyone agrees with this one. Except for the Devil. Or the Tower. Well, it's a creepy card for sure. What's this all about anyhow?

Named or unnamed, its still Death

The original trumps created during the Italian Renaissance were ALL unnamed and unnumbered. Everyone knew what the pictures meant, and what order they were supposed to be in. And that order of those trumps varied from city to city and country to country. You were just supposed to memorize the names and order that was in use at the place and time you were playing the game. And then there was no set content or number of standardized trumps until the 1700's or so.

Sigh. So around 1760 people started naming and numbering the trumps. Printing was all about words and numbers as well as pictures, so adding names and numbers showed the printers' full craft: pictures and words.

A Jester

Now in some places there was a superstition about the Death card. Some people were creeped out by it, and so they somehow agreed to keep it unnamed and unnumbered. All the other cards were named and/or numbered, and as Death was always depicted with a skeleton and a scythe, everyone knew what this image meant. And that superstition has carried over to modern times.

But is it worthwhile? Rider Waite names and numbers the Death card. Of course, it's using Roman numerals, so maybe that doesn't count as a real number. And we all know magic is real and there's nothing about it that derives from superstition. So this one is a silly superstition and can be safely ignored. I said so; it's in a book, so it has to be true. Very shiny.

The Fool must be unnamed and unnumbered. Alternatively the Fool must be numbered 0. Or sometimes 22. And it's supposed to be the first card in the deck. Or maybe the last of the trumps. Or placed between Judgment 20 and the World 21. All this tsuris about the Fool. I could go for the cheap joke and say it's all foolish, but I never stoop to cheap jokes. (Tell that to someone that believes it.)

If you read the previous paragraphs about the Devil, you know that originally the trumps were all unnamed and unnumbered. The Fool is special. Not creepy, but special. Mostly like special which is a PC (politically correct) euphemism for those people of less-than-full mental capabilities. In the Italian Renaissance, court fools could be people who had less-than-full mental capabilities, but who did and said funny things. They also prized people who were of less-than-full height—midgets or dwarfs in those days. Any person who could make people laugh, and they didn't worry about being PC then. Times were different and less enlightened in the Italian Renaissance.

Be that as it may, the Fool was another universally understood figure. He didn't need to be named, and where he appeared in the deck could be changed because the Fool was kind of an extra card. In the game of Tarot he is important, but he operates in a strange and unique way. In divination, he is also somewhat special, so where he appears in the order can vary from deck to deck. Even Eliphas Levi, Papus, Etteilla and Court de Gébelin couldn't agree on the Fool. So if those worthy sages couldn't, why should we? Yeah, this one doesn't really matter. Do what you want—I wash my hands of this one.

The Jester's wand

18 Lore About Decks

Tarot is part *of the Western European Occult Tradition only—nothing with any other ideas, symbolism etc. can ever be proper tarot.* There are decks out there using Japanese, Chinese, Indian, Persian, Native American, Incan, Aztec and many other cultures' symbolism and images for tarot decks.

Okay, the first part of this rule—*tarot is Western European*—is absolutely true. Wow! Two statements that are factually true in tarot lore. I'm astonished!

So because part of it is true, does it make the whole rule true? I have seen many of these decks, read with a few, and they all seem to work. But are they as 'authentic' as a Western European deck? Depends upon what you call authentic. Certainly these 'foreign' decks use images from cultures that never had tarot until the 20th century.

Non-Western decks

This boils down to a purist issue. Are you totally married to the Western European Occult Tradition and the idea that tarot is an integral part of that and that it can be valid for that tradition and no other? Of course the tarot cards originally came from India, brought by the Gypsies through Egypt... Yeah I know, it's not really true, but it's still so fun and romantic.

So the reality of the issue is that Western Occultism is an amalgam of various disciplines and bodies of lore, most of which is Western European, but some (most notably Kabbalah and Alchemy) are not. And the Theosophists brought in much Hindu lore. So if the Western European magical tradition isn't purely Western European in the first place, then why should you expect all tarot cards to be purely Western European? Think about it.

Tarot decks from non-tarot sources are wrong and non-magical. This refers to decks using artwork from sources other than art specially created for tarot decks. DaVinci, Botticelli, Klimt, Dürer and other artists have had some of their artwork made into tarot decks. But these images were not ever originally created for any tarot deck. So can these decks be magical and valid and real?

I won't dispute the quality of any of these artists. And DaVinci is magical—he invented helicopters and other neat stuff, so I guess his deck would be okay. I'm not an art historian, so I can't really speak about those other artists.

Again, this boils down to the purist issue. At least these artists are Western European, so there's more feeling of them being 'right' for tarot. And hey—I bet if they would have thought of it, they certainly would have done tarot decks. Salvador Dali did. And his decks are collectible and worth a whole lot of money, so it has to be a good thing.

And much of the art by these artists is out of copyright, so publishers don't have to pay royalties to an artist. More money for the publisher. Cha-ching!

Tarot decks that are not drawn are not magical or valid. Here we have the category of tarot decks created from photographs, collage, fabric (which is then photographed and that makes it doubly awful in this category), and anything else that isn't created from regular drawn artwork. And this should also most properly include decks that have some photographic elements, and some drawn elements.

Everybody knows photography steals your soul, and so photographic decks with people can possibly have souls in them. Maybe this is where the screaming souls when the cards burn comes from! I'd rather not read with a deck containing other people's souls—or even parts of souls in them. Sounds more than a bit creepy!

As to other media, well I don't know about that. I guess you'll have to work with it for yourself.

Now let's get real here—EVERY deck is photographed. Even if the original artwork is drawn, those original images are somehow photographed/scanned/rendered/computerized in the process of making a finished deck of cards. Remember, the magic is spritzed into the deck just before the cards are sealed in plastic, so all decks properly made are magic. I said so, it's in a book, and so it's true. Shiny, shiny, sterling research and reasoning.

A tarot deck must be created by one artist. Mixed art decks have no power. And a corollary rule—collaborative decks are crap.

There are a few decks that are true collaborations—every card is done by a different artist. In these decks, each card is distinct and no two cards look like they were done by the same artist—because they weren't. Now if you feel that makes for a deck with 22 or 78 (or however many cards there are) different energies, well then I bet you wouldn't want to read with that deck. Hey, if two decks put together is mixing energies and possibly dangerous—imagine the danger in a deck mixing 78 different energies. That would be a really big explosion for sure!

Collaborative decks are different. There are many decks around where two or three people collaborated on a deck. Maybe one or two people 'designed' the deck and decided what they wanted the cards to look like, and an artist worked to create their vision. The Rider Waite deck and Crowley's Thoth deck are two very famous collaborations. And everybody knows Rider Waite is the best, truest and most authentic tarot deck ever... Well it is the quintessential deck of the 20th century. So I guess collaborations are okay. It was just a corollary, so it isn't a real rule of lore anyhow.

You must create your own tarot deck, design and draw it yourself. No other deck can have any power for you. This one comes directly from the Golden Dawn, and other offshoot Ceremonial Magical Traditions. In the Golden Dawn, each initiate a was expected to create their own deck for themselves. It was to show off how much you learned about tarot and other magical stuff, and also because those groups were into doing everything the most thorough way anyhow.

You can buy a blank deck of tarot-sized cards, with one side not coated in plastic so you can draw your own deck. Pretty cool, huh? However, if everyone must make their own deck the people who make and sell tarot decks won't sell many decks (except for the blank ones). And it takes a whole lot of time and energy. Everyone is so busy these days, with the internet, twitter, Facebook and everything else you can spend your time with. So I would guess that unless you are a member of some Ceremonial Magic Tradition, you will just ignore this rule. I know I certainly do.

And I'm no great artist, so I wouldn't attempt it anyway.

DIGRESSION #6

This is the last digression, I promise.

What about all those different sizes of tarot decks? Time was, there were two sizes of decks—the regular playing-card sized deck, and then the tarot sized deck. And everyone knew that playing cards were for playing games, and tarot cards were for telling fortunes and nothing else, right? Yeah—that's the way it was. Everybody was happy and there were no problems.

Until Crowley's Thoth tarot was published on different sized cards. And mini-decks were created. Those are neat, because you can put a full tarot deck in your purse, and still have room for other stuff in there. Then the round Motherpeace deck came out, and all bets were off. Those cards are *round* for heaven's sake! How can you read reversals if the cards are round? Not to mention, how do you shuffle them? And then came other decks in various sizes and shapes. Most are rectangular, but some are more square, some are more elongated. There are the giant Rider Waite cards—about 4x7 inches—big enough that you can hold them up to a group and everyone has a good chance of seeing the image. There are also tiny decks with cards no bigger than your thumbnail. And most every size in between.

So nowadays decks come in many sizes. Rider Waite comes in something like 5 different sizes at present. I have heard no lore about the correct size or shape of tarot cards, but we all know it's rectangular. I mean really—round cards? That's just ridiculous.

End of Digression #6.

AFTERWORD

Here it all is. All the wonderful received tarot lore I could find (or invent) gathered together in one handy book. And almost 99% of it all debunked. Feels pretty good to get all that BS out there and name it for what it is—pure BS.

Now you may or may not agree with me about some or all of this BS. And in the end, that's the ultimate point of this book. If you feel your cards work better if you wrap them in a silk scarf when you're not using them, then go ahead and wrap them in that silk scarf. But hopefully you have thought about it, and not slavishly followed whatever you were taught/told/read/divined/whatever from whoever spreads this stuff.

And if you are upset and angry at me for daring to expose all the secrets of tarot lore—cheer up. Maybe my wicked ways will catch up with me and I'll be blown up or hauled away by the Tarot Police™. You have permission to dance on my grave, if that would make you feel better.

Dancing on Estelle's grave

Alternatively, if you know of some tarot lore that I have somehow missed, please tell me about it, and I'll research it and hopefully I can get that knowledge out there as well. I'm always collecting new and different tarot lore. It never stops, there's always something new coming down the pike. As long as new books and decks keep coming out, I suspect there will be more tarot lore also.

I do think the tarot is magickal and wondrous and can be a vehicle for divining the future, wisdom, self-discovery and meditation. There are literally thousands of decks out there, and every one of them was created by someone who wanted to tie into the world-wide mystique and romance of tarot. Some were created for divination, some for a gimmick, some for collecting as art, and some for whatever other reason the creator(s) had. The deck that started as playing cards for a specific game has literally spread all over the world, and is now a universal divinatory language.

Tarot has been a part of my life since high school. I started with a Rider Waite deck (still have it, too—though not the box it came in—that disintegrated long ago), then got a couple more, and once I decided to collect tarot, I went from something like 30+ decks to now over 700. I'm still collecting. I read with a group once a month—our monthly tarot get-together. And hopefully we can keep meeting as long as we are able. I teach tarot, and have several talks, from very beginning to the patented going through Auntie Estelle's drawers—bringing 150 or so decks for people to look at and enjoy and compare. Gotta love those plastic storage tubs.

Tarot has been a comfort, solace and joy in my life for over 40 years. I love finding a new deck, and going through each card, mentally matching it to the 'template' of Rider

Waite, and comparing/contrasting it to various other decks I have. I currently read with something like 5 separate decks—each has its own character and situation I use it for. There is no such thing as my 'favorite' deck, because there are about 20+ that I really love and think are just wonderfully neat. And there are some I still think are icky. And a whole lot of decks that fall somewhere in between on that spectrum. I have a favorite tarot publisher, and books and tarot authors I really enjoy.

The symbolism of Tarot, both trumps and the Rider Waite pips is a part of my personal mindset. I have been reading about and studying magical, esoteric and secret lore since I could read. I started with mythology, and kept going. Tarot came into the picture when I was in high school—I learned about it a couple years earlier but I got my first deck then. Astrology came first, but tarot is the second system I learned in my esoteric lexicon. And both are open-ended systems. A person can never know everything about either—they can be studied and worked with as long as a person wants to. There's always something new to be learned. Being a person who loves reading and learning and teaching, tarot is a great system for all of that.

However the pictures of tarot started, they have evolved into a coherent symbol-set that speaks to humanity across many cultures. Which means those symbols draw upon something deep within the human psyche, that is universal. And all the variations, gimmick or serious, also draw upon that deep psychological stuff that we can talk about, but can never really totally define. There should still be mysteries to Life, the Universe and Everything, and tarot is a part of all that. It makes being human more fun, IMHO.

I stated before, that I believe in writing about things

that haven't been done before. I'm not learned enough to have new theories about the cards themselves or their symbolism, or to design a new deck. But I do 'collect' tarot lore, and I do a talk about all the lore and how it's really just superstition and intimidation. (Don't tell the Tarot Police™.) So when someone said, "you should write a book about that"—well I did. Not the first time I heard that statement, and that other book is still around—thank you Paul—so I'll hope this one will last for a while also. And rather than beat people about the head and shoulders while passing on all the lore—as some authors can do when dispensing their version of THE TRUTH—I chose to use humor. Mirth and reverence, and when debunking BS, mirth is my tool of choice.

Hopefully people can still enjoy and revere tarot for what it actually is—warts of the made-up histories and all. And those made-up histories are certainly part of the mystery and romance of tarot—even if they were made up. But I prefer everyone also know the REAL history of tarot. It does not make it any less magickal and special. You can still tell fortunes with your tarot deck no matter which theory of history you subscribe to. And if knowing the truth spoils it all—well then I wonder how realistic you are about tarot and just how magical those cards can be for you. The cards are the same as they were before you learned the truth about the history, lore or whatever. Only your understanding and outlook has changed.

So lighten up—shuffle your deck, lay them out, and do a reading for yourself. Or a client. Or whoever. And remember, if you riffle shuffle, the magic will leak out! Shiny!

THE HIGH PRIESTESS

Glossary

Arcana—ancient, arcane. The two parts of a tarot deck are referred to as the Major Arcana and Minor Arcana.

archetypes—cultural or universal symbols which are understood by a majority to depict themes, stories and ideas. The tarot trumps are archetypes, as they are nearly universally recognized. Nowadays the trumps can mean different things than they did when they were created during the Italian Renaissance. Still, show anyone the Death card, and they will probably think it means death. That's an archetype.

Book of Thoth—alternate name for the 22 tarot trump cards, as used in a divinatory and esoteric manner. Named for Thoth, the Ancient Egyptian god of knowledge and learning, tying tarot in to the popular theory of tarot originating from Egypt.

Cabala—see Kabbalah

cartomancy—reading the future, or divination using cards. This can include tarot, but also playing cards, and many other decks of cards devised for various uses.

Celtic Cross—a particular spread for reading tarot cards. Supposedly invented in the Golden Dawn, and now a fairly universal spread, widely published. It has 10 cards (or 11 if a significator card is used), 6 in a cross pattern, and the last 4 in a line to the right of the cross. Some consider it the 'standard' spread for reading tarot.

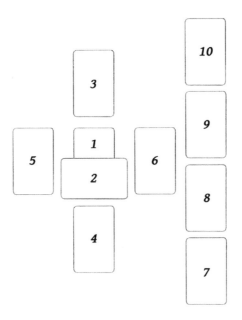

Celtic Cross spread

client—person who is getting a card reading. May or may not be for money.

court cards—AKA face cards. The suit cards depicting court figures. In tarot they are: the Page, the Knight, the Queen and the King.

divination—to commune with Deity by various means. Tarot cards are used for divination, both for telling fortunes and as a tool for meditation, introspection and esoteric learning.

element—in tarot the elements are the four classical

elements: fire, earth air and water. Some decks have a 5th element—spirit, metal, crystal or something else.

elemental correspondences—the four classical elements were assigned to the tarot suits during the Western Occult Revival. Not every group agrees on these correspondences. Cups are water, and pentacles or coins are earth. Most everyone agrees on those. Swords can be either air or fire, and wands can be fire or air. Rider Waite had swords as air and wands as fire, and as that is the most widely published deck, those are considered mostly standard correspondences. Other decks may change elements or add a 5th suit of another 'element', but that's not standard.

Etteilla deck—the first invented fortune telling deck, based upon a piquet deck, with the addition of an extra 33rd card, the Etteilla, which is the significator for the client. Etteilla created it, and later decks printed to his designs were made and sold. It was wildly popular; the deck sold with a booklet detailing the meanings of the cards, and how to read them. Thus, the cartomancer Etteilla invented a deck for fortune telling, widely popularized the practice of cartomancy, and created an industry of fortune telling in France from before 1770's and onward. The popular fad of cartomancy lasted until the 1820's in France.

face cards—see court cards

fortune telling—to tell the future using various means. Generally a derogatory term, indicating possible fraud, chicanery and possibly taking advantage of the weak and gullible. Also a term covering the reading of tarot cards and various other methods of divination, both spiritual and frivolous.

Grand Etteilla deck—Etteilla's second created fortune telling deck, based on a tarot deck, but the cards are numbered 1-77 plus the Etteilla—an extra card used to signify the client. This deck also became very popular with an accompanying booklet. Both these decks and his fame with fortune telling made Etteilla a rich and famous man. Both of Etteilla's decks were widely copied and imitated.

Hebrew Alphabet—the alphabet of 22 characters which is used in the Hebrew language, ancient and modern. There are also correspondences for these characters with numbers, which is an ancient use, and also later for the 22 tarot trumps, which had started by the time tarot was used for divination. In Kabbalistic teaching these letters also have special correspondences, but this has nothing to do with tarot as it originated. Not all esoteric scholars agree with which Hebrew letters are assigned to which tarot trumps.

historical deck—there are many tarot decks which recreate actual historical tarot decks—mostly those which were not originally used for divination. Many of these decks survive because they were painted, and they survived as art. Some historical decks are not complete—cards are missing. No decks of printed cards of any sort survive from before the 1600's, mostly because early paper was not made to last and the paper cards were fragile and wore out with use. Modern recreations of most all of the known historical tarot decks are readily available. Generally any tarot deck printed before about 1940 is considered historical.

Kabbalah—AKA, cabala, QBL, kabala, and many variant spellings—a Jewish learning tool, esoteric philosophy and correspondence method of equating everything in the Universe with 10 archetypal sephiroth, or spheres. This learning/teaching tool was correlated to tarot for magical and esoteric meanings by Eliphas Levi in the 1850's. Since then, it is a 'given' that tarot and Kabbalah have strong correlations and some falsely claim both originated together. They definitively did not.

Lenormand deck—a 36 card fortune telling deck as used by Mlle. LeNormand, a cartomancer who followed after Etteilla. It is based upon Etteilla's 33-card deck, with additional pictures and possible meanings. Mlle. Lenormand became rich and famous through her fortune telling skills before the French Revolution and afterward.

Little White Book, AKA LWB—a small book of card meanings included with a tarot deck inside the box the deck comes in. It usually has small print, may be stapled or accordion, and may or may not have meanings in several languages. Some people feel this LWB is not as useful or valid as a full-sized book about tarot card meanings, whether that book is deck-specific or just general. Because the deck and book together make for a very tight fit, the LWB sometimes ends up being discarded, so the cards can fit back in the box more easily.

magic—metaphysical, mystical. Stuff that comes about by means other than those that are explained by rational or scientific means. Any use of technology sufficiently advanced is indistinguishable from magic. Tarot cards are magic because they are used to tell the future and other mystical things. Tarot cards have magic in them, otherwise they could not be used to tell the future. Once the magic leaks out of a tarot deck, it is useless for telling fortunes.

Major Arcana—AKA the trumps or Book of Thoth. In

divination, the trump cards of a tarot deck take on special signification of a more esoteric and magical meaning. They are considered the seat of greater wisdom, hence the alternate titles of Major or Greater Arcana.

Here is a list of the Major Arcana, their French names and possible alternatives:

0 or unnumbered—The Fool, Le Mat. This card can be first of the trumps, the last, or placed between 20 and 21. This varies from deck to deck. Usually a person in motley dress stepping off a cliff, with a dog (or other animal) on his heels, sometimes biting the Fool as well.

1—The Magician, Juggler, Mountebank, Le Bateleur. A man standing at a table with a wand in his hand.

2—The High Priestess, The Popess, Pope Joan, Juno, La Papesse. A female sitting in front of a curtain with a book on her lap. This card has many variations, mostly from female religious figures, most of which were not considered 'legitimate' in Catholic Europe.

3—The Empress, L'Impératrice. A pregnant female figure seated with symbols of fertility and bounty surrounding her.

4—The Emperor, L'Empereur. A male figure seated with symbols of power and authority.

5—The High Priest, the Pope, Jupiter, Hierophant, Le Pape. A male figure seated with symbols of religious authority. Jupiter and Juno appear in decks after a Greek revival and lessening of religious authority in the 1700's.

6—The Lovers, L'Amoureux. Two or three figures surmounted by an angel. Sometimes modeled on Adam and Eve, sometimes as the temptation between virtue and vice.

7—The Chariot, Le Chariot. A wheeled cart drawn by 2 beasts—sometimes horses, sometimes sphinxes. A warrior rides in the cart.

8—Strength or Fortitude, La Force. A woman holding the mouth of a lion (or other beast) closed. Sometimes 8 is Justice.

9—The Hermit, L'Hermite. An old man standing on top of a mountain, looking downward with a lamp in his hand.

10—The Wheel of Fortune, La Roue de Fortune. A wheel surrounded by figures, some rising, some falling, some on top. The figures can be people, or mythological.

11—Justice, La Justice. A blindfolded woman holding a balance and a sword. Sometimes this card is Strength.

Originally in the standardized deck, 8 was Strength, and 11 was Justice. Then sometime between the late 1600's and mid 1700's one card printer in France reversed these trumps, making Justice 8 and Strength 11. Because this printer was very popular and many of their decks were sold, this reversal of order became 'standard', and other printers followed this new order. Later, after the mid 1800's, the reversal was discovered and Justice and Strength were restored to their original places, except by those who were accustomed to the new order.

12—The Hanged Man, the Traitor, Le Pendu. A man suspended upside down by one foot from a wooden structure. Sometimes he is naked, sometimes clothed. He usually has a peaceful expression on his face.

13—Death, La Mort, or unnamed and unnumbered "called" L'Arcane sans nom. A skeleton or cloaked figure with a scythe, usually mounted, with bodies around.

Originally all tarot trumps were unnamed and unnumbered;

a person just memorized their proper order and meanings to play the game. Eventually they were numbered and the images standardized. Death or 13 was considered unlucky, so in some decks this card was left unnamed and unnumbered, because the symbol of the skeleton or hooded figure carrying a scythe was universally understood. Some decks still follow this fashion, most do not.

14—Temperance, Tempérance. An angel. Sometimes this card is prudence, or faith.

15—The Devil, Le Diable. A demonic bat-winged figure seated, with two humans chained to the block the demon is sitting upon.

16—The Tower, The Tower/House of God, The Lightning Struck Tower, La Maison Dieu. A tower struck by lightning, partially destroyed with figures falling therefrom.

17—The Star, L'Étoile. A nude female figure pouring water into a pool.

18—The Moon, La Lune. A crescent moon overlooking a dog and a wolf, with a water creature crawling out of the sea, and a path leading up between two towers.

19—The Sun, Le Soleil. Two children in front of a big Sun or a child seated on a horse with the Sun behind.

20—Judgment, Le Jugement. People arising from coffins with an angel blowing a trumpet overhead.

21—The World, Le Monde. An androgynous figure in an oval, with a lion, an eagle, a bull and a man in the corners.

Mason, Masonic—a fraternal organization which started in the 1700's in Europe. Their activities and membership are secret, and among their many teachings are occult and metaphysical subjects. Many early students of the mystical and divinatory tarot from the 1700's to the early

1900's were Masons, and so tarot lore, teachings and symbology has a strong Masonic influence. Because of the secret nature of the organization, Masons have enjoyed a chequered reputation among various entities in the past and present. Some groups (most notably until recently the Catholic Church) have considered Masons anathema, others (like many of the founding fathers of the USA) have been Masons themselves, and welcome the organization.

Minor Arcana—AKA the suit cards. In divination the non-trump cards of a tarot deck which may or may not have special divinatory meaning. If they have divinatory meaning, they are considered lesser in import to the trumps, hence the alternate titles of Minor or Lesser Arcana.

non-standard tarot deck—many tarot decks have elements which make them non-standard. The most common variation is to change the court cards from Page, Knight, Queen and King, to other people significators. Some make the Page a Princess and the Knight a Prince. This gives gender balance, two male and two female cards. Mother, father, son, daughter is another option. Some add two female cards, a female page and a female knight card, adding 8 cards to the deck. There are many other people variants. Another variation is to change some trumps, which usually happens in decks not based on Rider Waite. Some people add extra trumps to the deck. There are decks with a 5th suit, adding 14 new cards. Some decks do many different variant things, adding court cards, adding trumps and adding extra cards as well. Purists consider any of these variants make the deck not true tarot, and won't use such decks. Other people welcome and embrace the changes. It's a matter of personal taste.

pictorial pips—in some tarot decks, each card, including the pips, has a special distinct picture relating to its divinatory meaning. The Sola Busca deck has pictorial pips, but it seems to be the only Renaissance deck like that. This fashion started more widely with game playing decks in Germany in the 1800's, and these pictorial decks came to be used for divination, and the practice of making the whole divinatory tarot deck pictorial was solidified with the Rider Waite Tarot, first marketed in 1909, and in print ever since.

pips, pip cards—the numbered suit cards from 1 or Ace to 10. Also a slang term used to describe divinatory decks with non-pictorial pips, that is, pips which only show the suit symbol in the correct number. 6 swords for the 6 of swords, 8 wands for the 8 of wands and so forth. There may be some extra decoration (like leaves or arabesques) on these cards as well as the 7 coins or whatever, but no other special distinct pictures apart from the suit symbols.

piquet, piquet deck—a specific deck of playing cards. 32 cards, 4 suits of pips—ace and 7-10—plus jack, queen and king. Usually a regular deck is used, removing the pips 2-6 from each suit. Used for the game of piquet and other games using this specific deck.

plastic—modern man-made material created in a laboratory using petrochemicals. Decidedly non-magical, and something you don't want to store your tarot cards in. Also a transparent somewhat waterproof material used to coat cards to make them more long-wearing and water resistant. Most all modern tarot decks are coated in plastic as part of their manufacturing process.

playing cards—a standard deck of cards, 52 cards in 4 suits of 13 cards each, 10 pips from Ace to 10 and 3 court cards, jack, queen and king. Used for playing games alone or in groups. Regular playing cards can be used for divination, but that doesn't make them tarot cards.

psychic reader—generally a person who reads tarot cards is just a reader or a tarot reader. The people who call themselves psychic readers are usually professional readers who may claim to rely upon psychic abilities, but who more commonly use confidence tricks to get money from their marks. Psychic readers use various means to tell the future, such as crystal balls or tarot cards. They may claim to be a medium and able to contact departed spirits, and may use spirit spelling. Some are legitimate. Some are not, and use their readings to gradually extort more and more money from their marks. These can be the storefront readers, not associated with a bookstore or any other business, and who are usually out to make as much money as they can, by whatever means they can devise. Many of these confidence people use the curse scam—they do readings or whatever, and it usually boils down to (after many readings and much money has been exchanged) a curse, which can be alleviated by drawing an amount of cash out of a bank, bringing it to the reader wrapped in a specific scarf or cloth, and the reader cleansing the money magically, thereby removing the curse. The wrapped package is returned, with the admonition, not open the bundle before a month (or more) has elapsed, or it will turn to ash, and the curse will return. When the person finally unwraps the bundle, they find a sheaf of cut newspaper and their money is gone. This is theft by swindle, considered fraud, and is a crime. It hurts legitimate readers, and is why many legitimate readers display a sign stating 'readings are for entertainment purposes only'. It protects them from the laws designed to protect the public from fraudulent readers. They are everywhere.

Generally, if a person uses the adjective 'psychic' before whatever they do—psychic reader, psychic astrologer, whatever—they are usually more shady than legitimate.

QBL—see Kabbalah

reader—person who tells fortunes with cards, or other method of divination.

reading—a session of divination where a reader offers tarot (or other) cards to a client, who shuffles the cards. The reader then lays the cards out in a pattern, and reads the meaning of the cards to the client. Also, any divinatory reading by whatever means.

reverse, reversal—a card which is turned upside-down, the image is reversed to the reader and/or client. Some readers read reversals differently from the card upright, some readers don't read reversals at all—they turn all cards upright. Some say read the cards as they lie. Some feel reversals change the meaning of the card, that is, making the meaning opposite from the same card upright. Some feel a reversed card has a separate meaning from the card upright, but it might not be opposite, or even have any connection to the upright meaning at all. There are a few round tarot decks which were specifically designed so as to be incapable of having reversals.

Rider Waite Tarot deck—the most widely published tarot deck, and the archetypal tarot deck of the 20th century. Designed by Arthur Edward Waite, and drawn by Pamela Colman Smith, it was first published in 1909 by Rider & Co. and has not been out of print since. It was the first widely distributed deck with fully pictorial pips, and is the template for many other decks. It is common when describing a deck to state if it is Rider Waite derived, if the images are similar to those in that deck. Some call it the Rider Waite Smith deck, thereby giving Pamela Colman Smith her due for drawing it. This deck comes in many sizes, and has several variants; Albano Waite, Golden Waite, Universal Waite and others.

round cards—supposedly originally all cards from India were round, as that was the shape of the paper they were printed upon. Some modern tarot and playing card decks are round. Motherpeace Tarot was the first widely distributed round deck—it was deliberately designed to be round so as to eliminate any reversals.

shuffle—method of mixing cards in a deck so as to randomize their order. There are many ways to shuffle cards, but you must never riffle shuffle your tarot deck or the magic will leak out.

significator—a card used to depict the client in a tarot reading. May be chosen according to various rules, or randomly drawn with the rest of the reading. Whether a significator is used depends upon the spread chosen for the reading. There are many conventions for choosing a significator. Using the Magician, trump 1 for a man, and the High Priestess, trump 2 for a woman is one traditional method. You can use the court cards, and choose a court card that corresponds to the client. A Page for a young person or child, a Knight for a young man, a Queen for a woman, a King for an older man. Which suit you choose depends on the coloring of the client, or their temperament or the reader's intuition. This is the method advocated with the Rider Waite deck. Or another card may be used at the whim of the client or reader.

silk scarf—many tarot authorities claim a tarot deck must be wrapped in a silk scarf to protect it from outside influences. The scarf may also double as a cloth to cover the table surface during a reading.

spread—a set pattern of laying out tarot cards for a reading. Each position has a meaning, and where the cards fall make up the reading as interpreted by the reader. There are many spreads, and making up new spreads is a fun tarot exercise.

standard tarot deck—a standard tarot deck has 78 cards: 56 minor arcana; 4 suits of 14 cards each—the pips numbered 1 or ace to 10 and the court cards, Page, Knight, Queen and King—and 22 trumps. Any deck which deviates from this standard pattern or number of cards is not considered a true tarot deck according to the purists.

suits, suit cards—the tarot cards that are not trumps are the suit cards. They are the pips, numbered cards from one or Ace to 10, and the court cards, Page, Knight, Queen and King. There are 4 suits in a tarot deck. Originally these suits were wands or staves, cups, swords and pentacles or coins. At time has progressed these suits have morphed into the common suits for playing cards we all know, clubs, hearts, spades and diamonds. Some European countries use other suit symbols; acorns, bells, shields, leaves and others.

symbolism—use of pictorial elements to signify ideas, concepts and lore beyond the symbol itself. Tarot uses symbolism widely, in each card and especially the trumps. The trumps themselves are strong symbols, which are almost universally recognized. Using art and drawings as mnemonics for wider concepts is the basis for using tarot as a tool for divination.

tarot—the name of a deck of cards and also a game played with said deck. The deck consists of 78 cards: 56 of which are the suit cards, 4 suits of 14 cards each from ace or 1 to

10, and 4 court cards, Page, Knight, Queen and King. The suits are hearts/cups, diamonds/coins, spades/swords and clubs/wands. Then there are the trump cards—22 in all. This deck started as a deck for playing a game, and has morphed into a deck used for divination or cartomancy—i.e. fortune telling. The game tarot has many variant names, tarocchi, tarok, trumps, triomps, triomphi, triumphs and other similar variants.

Tarot Police™—a group of people who police the correct use of tarot cards. They are a shadowy lot, never revealing themselves unless a reader profanes the use of tarot cards as laid down by received sacred wisdom. They can knock on a reader's door, and take their deck away if they are not using tarot correctly, and may also psychically brand them as a failed tarot reader, thereby making them incapable of reading tarot cards ever again. This is really bad, and so you'd better follow the rules, or they might show up at your door some dark night.

Theme deck—many tarot decks have been designed around themes. Decks like the Tarot of Baseball and the Baseball Tarot are two more prominent ones. There are decks about Gummi Bears, various Anime series and characters, Hello Kitty, Alice in Wonderland, Vampires, Zombies, Steampunk and on and on and on. These decks may or may not be created for readings—some are created solely as art for collectors. Some of the themes are more serious than others—Gummi Bear Tarot is a cute gimmick. It sells, for sure. Many of the Vampire themed decks are popular with the Goth-type crowd. There are decks using imagery from cultures which never had tarot before the 20th century: Japanese, Chinese, Islamic, Egyptian, Mayan, Incan, Celtic, Persian, Indian, Native American and so on. Makers of these decks use the template of tarot, borrow imagery from other cultures, and fit them to the cards, with changes where they feel it works for them. Whether or not these decks are considered true and proper tarot is in the eye of the beholder.

Tree of Life—a diagram used to help illustrate some concepts of Kabbalah, the 10 sephiroth or spheres, and the paths connecting them. Tarot trumps were assigned to these paths, thereby making the tarot more thoroughly connected to Kabbalah. Not every tarot scholar agrees with which trumps go with which paths, nor do they all agree on the assignment of the Hebrew letters either.

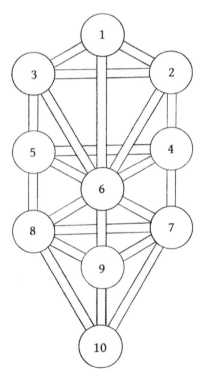

Tree of Life

trumps—AKA the Major Arcana. Originally added to a

standard playing card deck as an extra suit of permanent trumps for playing a card game. Nowadays, the extra cards which are considered more magical and more important in the deck. The original trumps were based upon imagery from mystery plays and pageants popular during the Italian Renaissance.

Western Magical Tradition—a group of teachings and practices which has evolved through the centuries. Originally based upon Ancient Greek and Roman esoteric books, as time went on, various people added to the lore. Magic, alchemy, astrology, kabbalah, divination and other practices are part of the Western Magical Tradition, though not all of those disciplines originated in the West. As of the late 1700's, tarot was added into that mix, first as reading with the 22 trumps only, and later reading using the whole tarot deck. Practitioners of this tradition through the last 250+ years have added to its lore and body of knowledge, usually by means of adding correlations between branches of learning. This is where the astrological and kabbalistic correspondences to tarot have originated.

Western Occult Revival—starting shortly after the Age of Enlightenment in the 1600's and at about the time of the Industrial Revolution in the 1750's, when all magical lore was abandoned wholesale in favor of science and the scientific method, there was a revival of occult knowledge and practice, as a reaction to the new science. Old lore and practice was revived, and scientific method was applied to ancient practices and formulae, resulting in a newer body of lore, based upon old teachings, but also adding new elements. Tarot was one of those elements added to all the old stuff. Without this Western Occult Revival, tarot might have languished and died as a mere fad, like that of French fortune telling. Now tarot is considered part of a larger magical and esoteric education, thereby assuring its place in modern metaphysical study.

BIBLIOGRAPHY

Amberstone, Ruth Ann and Amberstone, Walt, <u>Tarot Tips</u>, 2003, Llewellyn Publications

Decker, Ronald, DePaulis, Thierry and Dummett, Michael, <u>A Wicked Pack of Cards</u>, 1996, St. Martin's Press

Decker, Ronald and Dummett, Michael, <u>A History of the Occult Tarot</u>, 2002, 2008 Gerald Duckworth R& Co.

Giles, Cynthia, <u>The Tarot, History, Mystery and Lore</u>, 1992 Fireside Books

Hall, Manly P., <u>The Secret Teachings of All Ages</u>, 1928 The Philosophical Research Society, reprinted 1975 in Golden Anniversary Edition.

Kaplan, Stuart R. <u>The Artwork and Times of Pamela Colman Smith</u>, 2009, U.S. Games Systems, Inc.

Levi, Eliphas, <u>The History of Magic</u>, orig. 1859, translated by A.E. Waite, 1913, William Rider and Son, reprinted in facsimile by The Lost Library.

Mathers, S.L. MacGregor, <u>The Tarot</u>, orig. 1888, reprinted 1993, Samuel Weiser, Inc.